The Makeup of a Virtuous Woman

Keima A. Campbell

Proverbs 31:10
"Who can find a virtuous woman? For her price is far above rubies."

Keima A. Campbell

Unless otherwise indicated, Scripture verses are taken from The Holy Bible, English Standard Version® (ESV®), copyright © 2001 by Crossway, a publishing ministry of Good News Publishers. Used by permission. All rights reserved.

Verses marked MSG are taken from Scripture quotations from *THE MESSAGE*. Copyright © by Eugene H. Peterson 1993, 1994, 1995, 1996, 2000, 2001, 2002. Used by permission of NavPress Publishing Group.

Scripture quotations marked (NIV) are taken from the Holy Bible, New International Version®, NIV®. Copyright © 1973, 1978, 1984, 2011 by Biblica, Inc.™ Used by permission of Zondervan. All rights reserved worldwide. www.zondervan.com The "NIV" and "New International Version" are trademarks registered in the United States Patent and Trademark Office by Biblica, Inc.™

All the stories related in this book are true, but most names have been changed or omitted to protect the privacy of the people mentioned.

Cover by Designz by Kehmoi, Atlanta, Georgia

Copyright © 2014 Keima A. Campbell

All rights reserved. No part of this publication may be reproduced, stored in a retrieval system, or transmitted in any form or by any means-- electronic, mechanical, and digital, photocopy, recording, or any other-- except for brief quotations in printed reviews, without the prior permission of the author.

ISBN: 0615998003

ISBN-13: 978-0615998008

DEDICATION

This book is dedicated to any woman or young girl who has experienced struggle and adversity in their lives. You hold a very special place inside my heart. You are my ministry just as I am my ministry. I wrote this book so that you could know that God has not forgotten about you. He still loves you despite what trials and tribulations life has brought you through. You're beautiful. You're powerful. You're worthy to be loved and adored. Most of all you'll always belong to a loving and caring Father in Heaven. May the words of this book consume you and bless you on your journey after God's Everlasting Love.

CONTENTS

Acknowledgements i
Preface ii
Introduction vi

1	Connection of the Mind, Body, and Soul	1
2	The Bread of Life	24
3	Food For Thought	46
4	Primer	68
5	Concealer	84
6	The Foundation of Faith	107
7	Faith With Works	125
8	The Color of Virtue	149
9	Insight to See	173
10	To Speak Life	192
11	Fashioned by God	207

ACKNOWLEDGEMENTS

I'd like to first and foremost give thanks to God who is the leader of my life, my everlasting joy, and my Knight in Shining Armor. My mother Sheryl Campbell who has been my nurturer, protector, the one who guided and lead me in the right direction and showed me a whole lot of love. I'd also like to thank her for taking time out of her busy schedule to help with the cover of this book. It turned out awesome! I also want to acknowledge my Aunt Lisa Frank who is my prayer partner. We came up together one way and He molded us into women in another way. I'd also like to give a special thanks to the beautiful models my granny Odell Sallie Jones, my mother Sheryl Campbell, Aisha Stewart, Toya Abbott, Sadie Peters, Rosalvina Estrada, Stephanie Jones, Sandra Ray Parker, Lieu Nguyen, Stacie Flowers, Tina Campbell, Jennifer Lacour, Cynthia Salim Traylor, Denise Gaines-Wheeler, Wendi Strunk, Johnyette Sloan, Julie Martin, Porsha Carr, and Karen Gallardo. Each one of you has brought something unique and beautiful to the cover and I thank you for being a part of this project. To my friends and family who have supported me throughout my writing journey, my daughters Aminah and Ariyah Cottle for always having my back, my grandparents Russell and Sallie Jones, my brothers Kevin Jordan, Darrien Dean, Lil' D and Devontair "Vonnie" Jackson, my baby sister Tierra Jackson, my son McCoy Jones and baby girl Miriam Finch, Joe and Tania Campbell my aunt and uncle, Uncle Derek, my aunt and uncle Yolanda and Milton Carr, and anyone else who has encouraged and believed in this ministry God has given me. To all of my fans who have stuck with me throughout my transition from writing secular books to coming into what God has prepared for me, I truly feel blessed to have you in my corner and thank you.

PREFACE

Me? No God. You can't possibly be serious. This isn't correct. Maybe I'm hearing things. No, I get it; I must be losing my mind. I'm not in a position to tell anyone about Your goodness and mercy. Do You realize who You're asking to do this? I'm nobody! No one has seen me on T.V., I don't have an endless amount of cash, I drive a minivan, and I have four children with three different fathers! Who in their right mind is going to listen to me?

I was raised in a single parent home; my own father didn't want me. All those men I've had sex with, the street lifestyle I idolized, none of that represents You even a little bit. What about the time I tried to commit suicide? Or did you forget about all the degrading things I've done in the name of money? I'm not worthy to write this book. I know there's someone else for You to choose Lord. Someone who's better than me.

These were the excuses I used trying to run away from what God had placed heavily on my heart. The enemy was telling me that I was not worthy to write a book about Our Father. The enemy wanted me to believe that I couldn't go from writing urban fiction and erotica to spreading the Gospel of Jesus Christ through my gift. For months I wrestled with that small voice inside of me urging me to start on this journey of enlightenment.

His voice became a little bolder as He laid it all out for me to understand. He told me that the time was now to truly experience God for myself. His

Spirit acknowledged that it was time to heal and move forward into all that God had for me. He showed me the beauty of trials and tribulations. I was assured that all the hell I went through was not in vain. My own free will had positioned me to tell this story.

So many women needed to know that all things work for the good of those of us who love the Lord. It didn't matter how many mistakes we'd made, God still loved us and we are all usable. I came into a realization that my body was the sacred temple of God and that the Holy Spirit would work through me so that His Divine Will over my life could be done. He was who made me somebody, not being famous, driving fancy cars, or living the picture perfect life. Yet, He still had a place for me. Not even those whom I'd deemed better than me could deny the greatness that He'd placed inside of me. It wasn't just about me but about all of us. His wisdom showed me that as long as we moved according to His Will everything would fall into place.

As God convicted me to write this book all of a sudden I felt this overwhelming feeling of shame and joy all in one. I closed my eyes opening my mouth confessing everything I'd ever done in my life as hot tears slid down my face. For the first time in my life I took full responsibility for every decision I'd made. I no longer blamed everything on my circumstances or other people. I was saying, "I did this and I'm sorry. I want to walk away from sin forever. I never want to make you unhappy with me again Father God."

I cried out to Him for a very long time. Everything I could think of that was disgraceful I boldly brought it before Him. The more I spoke the less shame I felt. The less shame I felt the lighter I became. The lighter I became the more open my heart was to receive. That might sound crazy but it literally happened exactly that way.

From that moment forward, God started moving at a very rapid pace in my life. He was picking me apart piece by piece and rebuilding me into the woman He knew me to be. He removed everything dark and illuminated me with the Holy Spirit. Things I had been holding on to for years, I was able to completely let go of. He told me that He had already set the platform for me to spread the "Good News" to other women who had lost their way.

He'd removed all my insecurities and enhanced my talent as a writer so that I could do His work. He was just waiting for me to let Him in and was very pleased with me when I did. In that moment I began to cry harder because although I know that He had set me on this sacred path, I had a revelation that this process would be a very humbling experience to a very proud woman. The shame and guilt that crumbled me as a child into my adult life would be on paper. I was going to write a book putting all of my transgressions, all of my sins, my deepest darkest feelings, in front of a multitude of people. They would either see the work that God had done in me or would judge me.

As frightening as that sounded I wasn't afraid. The burdens of my past had literally been lifted from me and I surrendered placing all my trust in Him. The Makeup of a Virtuous Woman would help so many women in this world that were hurting. The Spirit of God moved me to read the Word and the more I was fed the more knowledge and truth flowed from my entire being. I received closure to things I'd held on to for more than thirty years. Finally I was filled with a peace I didn't know existed.

I'd been writing since the 6th grade and would never have thought it would lead me to God. The things I used to write gave me a temporary outlet for the sorrow I harbored deep inside but never actually healed me. In writing this book however, I'd been renewed. Those things that caused me pain gave me great joy because I knew that it was Him who carried me through it all.

I knew He was doing a great deal of work inside of me because people began to flock to me. When they came to me it wasn't all smiles and happiness they came to me for guidance and prayer. They needed the God in me to heal them. Once, I had given them what they needed they would thank me. I'd look at them shaking my head, no, and then give Him all the glory and praise because I knew it wasn't me that was helping them. It was the God in me that had done the work. The more people, He sent to me, the more convicted I became. I felt this overwhelming urge to glorify His Name not just when His works were obvious but in everything.

The Spirit began to speak to me daily as I walked with Jesus. This relationship led me to pray longer and harder. The love and beauty that had manifested inside of me was spilling over encouraging me to consider my overall health. My family and I began to focus on living a healthy lifestyle by working out and eating foods that healed our bodies. Just like that He made me aware and alert of things I never deemed as important.

The peace that I had always been looking for had finally found me or maybe I had found it, either way I was grateful. His grace, love, mercy, kindness, and nurturing had changed me for the better. I knew that as a woman of God it was my duty to answer the call He had on my life and to tell my story. My story is the story of many woman and God wants you to know that it is not over. He will free you from any bondage that is hindering you from receiving all that He has for you.

He will give you peace, joy, happiness, hope, understanding, and most of all love. All you have to do is allow Him to. He is waiting on you the same as He waited on me with open arms. God loves all of you and so do I.

INTRODUCTION TO HOW TO USE THIS BOOK

This book wasn't written to tell you exactly what to do to become one with God. I say this because we all have to take personal accountability for our own life and be prepared to walk with God in the way that He intended for us to do so. This walk isn't easy and in order for us to successfully walk with the Lord we must be prepared to let ourselves go. The spiritual process of healing can be just as painful as recovering from a physical injury. The ultimate result however is peace beyond all understanding and true unconditional love.

In dying and becoming reborn in Jesus Christ we finally find our comfort zone. We stop living to die and are living to live. Our spirit is renewed and we can rejoice in the life that God has intended for us all along. There are no worries when we fully submit to Him because we know who we belong to and understand who we are in Him. Our minds, bodies, and souls are nourished and made acceptable to receive our very own portion of the Holy Spirit in Its' highest capacity. We are able to function on a higher level of spirituality, sharing the love and hope that God has given to us, and to others who are in need.

God has strategically placed each and every one of us on our own personal path. The Makeup of a Virtuous Woman will show you some simple steps that I used to get in alignment to do God's Will in my life. Each chapter is extremely important in building your personal relationship with God. In order for the

Holy Spirit to consume us we have to let go of anything that is keeping us bound to an ungodly lifestyle. By allowing the light to shine through you, you'll overcome even your darkest hour.

I have included personal stories from my own life in every chapter. These chapters also describe our responsibilities as virtuous women according to Scripture, as well as how the Word of God applies directly to our lives. When reading Scripture it is important to have a Bible available for your own personal reference. There may be times when the Spirit moves you to go even deeper than what is in this book. That's fine because when that happens there will be revelation for you in that area of your life. Trust the Spirit as it moves within you.

Praying and meditating on the Word is an essential everyday practice. Speak God's Word over you and your family. There is power in Scripture. Each day we will grow a little more into our true selves. We will find that we have become better, mothers, daughters, friends, cousins, aunts, wives, and women in general over the next several weeks.

Journaling is also a very important aspect of growing spiritually. Each day we will take time out of our busy lives to reflect on our spiritual needs. It can be something that happened on that day, something that's resurfaced from your past, or you can journal about a situation you see in your future. At the end of each chapter there is a journaling guideline for each day of the week to help you with the process.

Please remember not to rush yourselves through this book. This is a process and if you feel you have not learned enough in any given chapter to move on by all means stay where you're at and dig deeper. In digging deeper we become more intimate with Him and that intimacy provides us growth. We recognize where we are and where we're going. Once we're heading in the right direction, we then begin the transformation process of sinner to saint.

At any time please don't become discouraged because you feel off track. Know that the relationship you have with Our Father is not going to be exactly like mine. He will work in our lives in different ways sometimes and there's nothing wrong with that. Stay faithful and trust His Word. It took me years to finally begin to comprehend what a true relationship with God consisted of.

You may find some information to be repetitive however repetition is necessary when renewing the mind, body, and soul. For example, we do not lose weight, tone our bodies, and get fit after one day of exercise. It's a process. We don't pass exams by hearing or reading information one time. We study that information prior to taking the exam in hopes of getting an A. The same rules that apply to our physical lives also apply to our spiritual.

This book was written from a Christian standpoint but I truly believe that every woman from every walk of life can benefit from the information it contains. We are ALL His daughters. Contrary to what others may believe or say, He is waiting for women of all religious backgrounds and even those who are not religious to come to Him and surrender. I encourage you to try Him. I'm fully confident that your life will forever be changed. Now is the time to allow God to live within you. You are worthy and He is worthy to be praised. Let's begin this journey with a prayer and an exercise to open our minds, bodies, and souls.

Father God we come to you today in search of answers. Answers that will help us unleash the true meaning of our lives. We ask that You unleash all that You have been holding onto for us so that we may come into our full potential as women of God. We know that You are the sole source of our happiness, love, joy, peace, and hope. We need You at this time to make us whole, raise us into better women, mothers, daughters, wives, sisters, granddaughters, cousins, friends, human beings Father God. You are our only hope in releasing us and healing us from the pain of our past present and future. Open our minds Dear Lord so that we are able to receive Your message as we begin to live our lives according to Your Word. You have placed a great responsibility upon us Father God, as women we are bearers and teachers of the children and ministers to other women, we are the determining factor that our children grow up knowing You, believing in You, trusting You, having faith in You and living a lifestyle that glorifies and magnifies Your Holy Name. We know Father God that You are not a respecter of persons so what You do for one of us You will do for all of us. Teach us to walk like Jesus Christ, fill us with so much of Your light that there is no darkness left. Allow us to become perfected in You

Lord God. When we make mistakes Father God help us to not become discouraged but help us to see that through our trials and tribulations You are there to give us victory! Allow us to feel Your presence guiding us in everything that we do. Use us as a vessel to bring Your Will into fruition. You are so worthy to be praised Lord God; we lift up Your Holy Name. When we are hurting Lord God, let us see that You are our Comforter, when we struggle to make ends meet Lord let us not worry because You are our Provider, when we are afraid allow us to trust You as our Protector, our Warrior, our Shelter from the storm. Guide us so that every word that we speak will be according to Your Divinity. We know that Your way reaps many blessings and favor. We ask that You give us a true understanding of our lives as we face the situations of the world Father God. We come to You right now fully submitting and open to all You have for us. We ask that you take us and make us new again as You lead us only into Your ways and shield us from all things that are not of You. In Jesus name we pray.

Amen

Answer the following questions to the best of your ability, being honest and true to where you are in your life right now. Write the answers down in your journal. (*Hint: Try to answer these questions as honest as possible you will be asking yourselves these questions again at the end of this book.*)

- Who am I?
- Who do I hope to become?
- What do I think I will gain from this book?
- What are the goals I will set for myself to

become a better me?
- When will I start transforming my life?
- When do I hope to start seeing the results of this transformation?
- Where in my life will these changes take place?
- Where will I go from here?
- Why do I feel the need to make changes in my life?
- Why is it important that I have a core set of values, standards, and morals?
- How do I represent myself as a virtuous woman now?
- How will I represent myself as a virtuous woman in the future?

The Makeup of a Virtuous woman

Connection of the mind body and soul
(1)

Under Attack

At the age of 15 I was much like any other 15 year old little girl, thought I knew it all and didn't believe I had to listen to anyone. My mother would say, "You're transitioning into becoming a woman. You're not quite old enough to do the things you want to do but you aren't young enough to be treated like a little girl anymore either. Give it time you'll get there. These years will determine if you'll take the right path or the wrong one." I thought she was full of it, she didn't know a thing about my life or what I was going through.

Even earlier than that I'd started walking down the wrong path, but at 15 things really began to pop off. My mind and heart were surrounded by a stone covering much like the outer layers that form a pearl. Life was turning into one big cancer and it all started with one of the most violent attacks on my mind to date.

My mother had just started another new relationship with a man whose presence seemed to make me anxious and uneasy. One night when he was visiting, I had this overwhelming urge to get him out of our lives for good. So, I grabbed a knife from the kitchen and slowly made my way to the back of the house towards my mothers' room. I'm unsure what I'd planned to do but I know my intentions weren't good.

I stood in front her doorway gripping my weapon as tightly as I could, my breathing shallow and erratic. I remember something in my head screaming, "DO IT! DO IT!" I felt this rage building inside of me. It felt as if I was bursting out the seams of my very existence. When I couldn't hold back any longer I lifted my foot pushing it hard into the wooden frame. The force was so strong it knocked the door nearly off the hinges allowing me to slowly step inside the room.

I stood there staring at them, knife in hand, my rage momentarily satisfied as the look of embarrassment, fear, even terror spread across their faces. As quickly as the kick released the rage, it began to become a rapid boil inside of me once again. I'd never felt that way before and I knew that if I stayed a second longer my life would forever be changed. I thank God for saving a small piece of sanity for me in that moment.

I turned around bolting through the house back towards my bedroom. I walked hurriedly dropping the knife off in the kitchen as my hands shook uncontrollably. When I reached my bedroom I began to tear it apart because I was unable to contain the anger I'd felt. I had visions of myself holding the knife covered in blood smiling and laughing aloud. Until this day I have no real explanation as to why I acted out like I did. It was like I was under some sort of demonic spell. I'd had violent outbursts many times over the years, but never to that extent.

When my mom walked into the bedroom to see what I'd done she too became enraged. I lay across my bed expressionless, trembling on the inside as she started throwing things around my room as well. I recall looking at her and feeling joyous. I wanted to smile as big as I could because I was happy she was as angry as I was. My face however, remained stoic. I didn't regret what I'd done. There was no remorse for what I wanted to do that night.

She sensed the spirit that had overcome me. It was so strong she literally feared what could happen if I stayed in her home that night, so she gathered my things and drove me to a mental institution. I felt so betrayed at that time. In my mind nothing was wrong with me, everything was wrong with her and her "man". I didn't need to be admitted into a mental institution. Only "crazy people" went to places like that and I wasn't crazy. If anyone needed to be admitted into a psychiatric facility it needed to be "her" and "him". I was perfectly fine.

Then my mind started to do those things that it had always done to me. It told me that my mother didn't really love me. No one did for that matter. She was my enemy and it wasn't the last time she'd betray me. She'd abandoned me for a man that she'd just started dating. I was only there taking up space, she didn't need me, and I didn't need her either. My mind convinced me I couldn't trust her with anything anymore and that I was on my own.

My time in the psychiatric hospital is somewhat of a blur. There are however, some things that I remember quite vividly. At night we were locked in our rooms, with no access to pens, pencils, notebooks, or anything that they felt we could harm ourselves with. I hated the fact that I couldn't write. Even if I crumbled up every piece of paper I poured my pain on to, it would help in that moment and I could relax, maybe even sleep.

They would distribute medications throughout the day trying to keep us in a state where we were easiest to deal with. I didn't need the medication but they'd never given me the chance to prove that I wouldn't be a "problem". I guess they didn't really have a choice considering the violent outburst that got me locked up in the first place. None the less that's what I felt. I'd watched enough movies to know how to pretend as if I was taking medications. I refused to swallow those meds and play a part in that, "zombie psychiatric patient" movie.

I distinctively remember an older woman who took her medication faithfully. She had mentally given up on herself. I don't know what her story was but I remember my heart being very heavy for her. I knew her mind had taken on a life of its' own placing her in a world of darkness, despair, and hopelessness. She'd sit in this chair for hours on end holding a cup of coffee, shaking, never taking a sip, as she stared out into space. She did this every single day. I didn't want to be her; I didn't want to completely lose control of my mind.

I've never forgotten that woman and I say a prayer for her anytime my thoughts take me back to that dark place. Mental illness? How do we get to such a place as this? How can we not have control over our very own minds? What if there is no such thing as "true mental illness"? What if the cure for not just mental illness but all illnesses and diseases starts within you? What if it starts with believing and trusting the Word of God?

I'm not in any capacity encouraging anyone who is under the care of a medical professional to stop seeing him or her. I am suggesting however, that you begin to take an active role in working with your healthcare provider to heal yourself. If God said that we are healed because of Jesus Christ being wounded and dying for our sins then why can't we be healed from everything including mental illness?

1 Peter 2:24 (ESV) "He Himself bore our sins in his body on the tree, that we might die to sin and live to righteousness. By His wounds you have been healed." It's important that we believe His Word. A disease of the mind is merely a spiritual battle. What happens to us physically is the outcome of the battle that is going on inside of us spiritually. Our physical bodies react to the spiritual warfare that is taking place deep inside of us. The easiest place to attack a person is in their minds. Why? Every action starts with a thought. If you can think it, you can do it. If the enemy can change our mindset he can ultimately change our lives.

Now that I understand the true meaning of being a woman I can reflect back on this time with a different outlook. This was one of those life altering moments in regards to my relationship with my mother. Although she had always taken care of me and been the best mother she knew how to be, I now know that her admitting me into the mental institution had caused me to hold a grudge against her. My mind playing tricks on me led me to believe that she could no longer be trusted.

Finding the Beginning

Walking with Christ forced me to come to terms with everything ungodly inside of me. I had to break down every moment no matter how trivial I thought it to be and search for the truth behind it. ***John 1:1 (MSG) "The Word was first, the Word present to God, God present to the Word. The Word was God."*** In order for me to start the healing process that would ultimately release me from my bondage I had to do several things. I had to start from the beginning to find the root of my pain.

The saying, "You must first know where you've been in order to know where you're going," is a very true statement. In the beginning we were all with God but what exactly happens or starts the chain of events that separates us from Him? Sometimes we have been dealing with a certain emotion for so long it becomes a part of us. We have to go back as far as we can remember to get to the root of our problems. Sometimes we may not know where to begin, but we know the pain is there.

You see, I was conceived when my mother was nineteen years old. Hearing the story of my conception and even my birth for that matter has always been painful for me to relive. For as long as I could remember my mother always told me the truth. Well at least the truth as she saw it. There are always two sides to a story and then there is what really happened minus ones perception. To sum it all up the extent of the relationship my mother had with my father was all sexual. After a small amount of time of them being together intimately my mother found out she was pregnant.

I'm not sure of the dialogue that took place between this man and my mother but from what I know he didn't want her to keep me. You see the problem was he was married at the time and felt strongly about keeping his marriage together. He was willing to do anything including pulling a gun on my mother threatening to end both of our lives to do just that. That was the last time she saw him in more than twenty years.

I can't fathom what could have possibly been going through his mind at the time but I know the pain his actions caused me to feel. For a long time, I saw my existence as God's one big mistake. No one could have told me otherwise. I mean why else would a man want to kill me and my mother while I was still in her womb?

Maybe I was too young to hear that truth about my life but none the less I was given it at around age of 6 or 7. To be honest I didn't know how to really receive it. Mama tried to lighten the force of the pain that smacked me in my gut by saying things like, "I refused to abort you or I loved you from the first moment I saw you." Those words came directly from the bellows of her soul. As a mother of four I understand where she was coming from now, but growing up, it never registered.

With all those affirmations coming from her I still felt as if I was doomed from the beginning. I was literally born in sin. I wanted to know what I had done that was so wrong that no one wanted to love me. My biological father not loving me turned into everyone else hating me. I was too afraid to ask my mom how she really felt about me because I thought that I was supposed to love her and it didn't matter if she loved me back or not. I mean after all, she hadn't aborted me. That should've been enough for me to feel grateful to her for.

I felt heartbroken on a daily basis, but overtime I was able to smile even through the excruciating pain of truly believing I was unlovable. The feeling of having my heart ripped out of my chest is a feeling I knew all too well because there was never a time I felt complete. There were so many sleepless nights because of this heartbreak I assumed I was destined for. My mind told me that I was nothing but the illegitimate child of two people who didn't care enough to be together for me. I would never amount to anything because I was nothing. My heart confirmed these thoughts by giving me these feelings of despair and loneliness.

The absence of love, I'd been exposed to since I was in my mothers' womb overcame me. Every feeling of abandonment, fear, and lack of love she felt during her pregnancy she had unknowingly passed down to me. Because of this I'd always had this insecurity in relationships. As an adult when people told me the stories about how I cried uncontrollably as a baby when my mother was gone caused me to wince in pain. I knew that it was not about me being spoiled. It was more about me feeling abandoned. It also confirmed the truth about this spiritual battle we're on. We are fighting for our lives even as infants.

The biggest problem however, with most of our battles is that we aren't able to recognize that we are in a war. I'd walked into a warzone just from being born and was never equipped for the battle. I didn't realize there was anything wrong and remained under constant mental attack and losing. The more spiritual battles I lost the more mistakes I made, and the more mistakes I made the more my heart would break. And as my heart shattered I spiraled out of control.

Love My Flesh

At 13 years old life as I knew it took a drastic change. I went from being teased on a daily basis about being overweight to the majority of the boys lusting over me. Puberty had provided me a power that I never knew I had. I mimicked my mother and aunts, adding pieces of myself as I went along making a completely new me.

The beautiful and confident person on the outside hid the immature little girl who was looking for love on the inside. I became two people in one, developed an alter ego, multiple personality. Not just the boys started to notice me but the men did too. They wanted me and I loved every minute of it. I soaked up the attention like a sponge, marveling in the fact that a man was paying me attention. I craved those ravenous eyes taking in my beauty. I needed that from them, wanted that from them. I needed that lust to feel like love. At least that's what my heart and mind told one another.

So the day that he approached me was very much welcomed. I was walking to the gas station when he pulled up beside me licking his lips and staring me down. It didn't matter that his eyes never met mine just his admiration of my body was enough for me. He was the very first one to approach me. He was the one who opened the door for all the others. We exchanged pager numbers and I felt like I had really accomplished something in grabbing his attention.

I fought with myself trying to decide if I would be the one to page first. In the end I decided to let him contact me, after all he was the one who'd flagged me down. By the time I got back from my walk he'd beeped me and I was grinning from ear to ear. When we finally spoke he wasn't short on compliments. He made me feel like he really cared and his interest alone had my full attention. I just knew I could make him love me, especially now that I was "beautiful." *If only my father could see how pretty I was he would love me too.*

I kept our relationship a secret because with him being 21 years old I thought my mother wouldn't understand the bond we had. The more we talked to each other the more I felt like I wanted to give myself to him fully. I wanted to become intimate with him and thought that was the best way to show him I loved him. When we were around each other I never noticed that he didn't look at me like I looked at him. My eyes were filled with hope and love but his consisted of pure lust with no intentions for a future with me.

None the less he was who I believed would change my life. He would give me the love that my father and stepfather were incapable of giving me. He was a man, my man. It didn't matter that he had a child by a woman his age or that word around town was he was still sleeping with her and a couple other females. I knew he loved me. He had to love me no one said the things he said to me just because. There had to be something behind his words.

The day came when I would be able to show him just how much I cared. We were together, alone, and I was ready to give him what I thought would make him stop dealing with all those other girls. Although I wanted it I was afraid. When he started to kiss me and caress my body, my young mind told me that this was right. I never stopped to think or even cared about what a man in his 20's had in a common with a 13 year old little girl.

When the excruciating pain of losing my virginity began to grip my body he could feel me stiffen. For a brief moment I thought about telling him to stop. But, I quickly asked myself what if he didn't want to stop? What if he became angry and continued to do it anyway? Or worse what if he stopped liking me?

He began to softly whisper into my ear walking me through the entire process. I wanted to scream, push him off of me, and run out of the room, but I wanted him to love me more than I wanted the physical pain to stop. So I held my breath, closed my eyes, and allowed it to happen. Despite the physical pain I felt in the moment, I was defining my place in his life. At least that's what my childish thoughts and confused heart had me to believe.

After that night our relationship changed drastically. His phone calls and pages were almost nonexistent. I knew that things had changed but my heart wouldn't let go. When he completely stopped returning my pages and phone calls altogether I was devastated. I'd ask myself, was there something wrong with me? Was I not pretty enough? Maybe I really didn't deserve to be loved. The seed was growing in that moment. Being abandoned by my father while in the womb is when the seed was planted. Losing my stepfather to divorce had watered that seed, but this situation was causing it to blossom.

There were many more after him. Each beginning and ending in a similar way with me hurt and asking why. After a while the pain became what was expected and every "relationship" I went into I'd prepare myself to be hurt. With each break up I became a little more hardened until I could no longer feel the pain. I was numb to that kind of pain. The hurt had turned into anger. I had no compassion for men. I hated them. Just as they had made me feel like I was only good for sex I used them in the very same way. Sex and money was all it boiled down to but over time even that became burdensome.

Living with a heart of stone took a toll on my body over the years. I was physically and emotionally unable to love and was living a very lonely life in terms of companionship. I was drowning in a sea of violent waves. The agony of heartache had consumed me. But God said, **Jeremiah 17:9 (NIV) "The heart is deceitful above all things and beyond cure. Who can understand it?"** Was my heart deceiving me? Or did I really feel these things? Had I ever been in love with these men that I believed to have broken my heart? Or was this all just a figment of my imagination? What was love anyway?

One day everything hit me as I stared at myself in the mirror. I was looking into the eyes of a woman that I didn't recognize. It was my face and my features, but there was a face behind the face that made everything distorted. It was the mask of hatred.

Every piece of me became ugly because of the hate that harbored itself inside of my soul.

As I stared at myself in the mirror one single tear fell down my cheek. I wanted to turn away in shame but I didn't. I stayed staring at that person in the mirror and that one tear became two, and soon a multitude of tears cascaded down my face. I stood there whimpering and those whimpers turned into heavy sobs. I felt as if I was crying out my very soul. It had been years since I had cried for myself. Once the flood gates were opened I couldn't stop.

I screamed out allowing my pain to be heard. Although there was not one audible word spoken in that moment I was calling out for God's Love. I was asking Him to love me and to come save me from myself. In that moment I realized I had absolutely no clue as to what love meant. I wasn't sure how it felt, how to receive it, or how to really give it for that matter. I was a mother and didn't even know how to truly love my own children. Those tears were asking God to show me how to love unconditionally. They were asking Him to show me to love like Jesus Christ.

Watering the Mind, Body, and Soul

Almost immediately I was led to my bible where God began to show me where to start my journey. You see although I had been saved I had no idea of what it meant to be delivered or of how to be in communion with God. I didn't have a clue about the importance of the body in regards to our souls. The Lord showed me that our bodies were made solely for the purpose of communion with our Creator. They were to be inhabited by the Holy Spirit so that we could complete His Will here on earth.

Just like every other plant and animal our bodies needed to be fed and watered for nourishment and growth. Not just physical nourishment and growth but spiritual as well. You see if we do not eat and get proper nutrition our bodies began to die. This holds true for our souls as well. If we do not consume the Word of God our souls will start to wither away.

We develop this feeling of emptiness and begin to question our very existence. But God, made it so our souls could be nursed back to health. Now when I had asked God to show me to love like Jesus, He started in me with the basics. The things that most of us take for granted and don't even realize are an important part of being in good spiritual health.

1 Corinthians 6:19-20 (ESV) "Or do you not know that your body is a temple for the Holy Spirit within you, whom you have from God? You are not your own, for you were brought with a price. So glorify God in your body." Scripture goes even further to say in, **1 Corinthians 3:16-17 (ESV) "Do you not know that you are God's temple and that God's Spirit dwells in you? If anyone destroys God's temple, God will destroy him. For God's temple is holy, and you are that temple."**

This to me has been the single most important piece of information in my spiritual journey. All this time I had been believing that I had to go to church to have a relationship with God. I thought that the only way I could have a "God Experience" was when I walked through the church doors, cried listening to the music, and received the Word from my pastor. When I left it was back to the "real world", the godless world and all was fair game.

I'd found that we didn't belong to ourselves we belonged to God. That meant every piece of us was His all the time. When I read this Scripture I began to sit back and really think about a lot of the choices I'd made. I had tattooed my body, eaten foods that contributed to me being overweight, physically and verbally fought others, sat around doing nothing but destroying the physical vessel that harbored the Holy Spirit. I had taken an active role in destroying the temple of God without even knowing it was His temple. When He showed me this I bowed to the ground in repentance. I had to ask for forgiveness and thank Him for showing me the Truth.

For so long I thought that doing these things were "normal" when in fact this was abnormal behavior. When we are following Jesus Christ our minds become alert and aware of what is good and bad. We are able to think clearly in terms of the spirit and in return we physically do what is required of us in order to be filled with the Holy Spirit of God. We take care of our physical bodies so that the Spirit of God can work through us in its greatest capacity. When our minds are clean, it ensures our bodies are clean. If our bodies are clean our souls are clean and able to connect with the Spirit of the Lord.

Our souls are what harbor our thoughts, feelings, and emotions. Those thoughts, feelings, and emotions are what will connect us with the Spirit of God or separate us. I'd never really taken time out to feed my soul. As I developed the habit of reading the Word of God, speaking the Word of God, praying, and meditating on the Word of God my soul became nourished. My soul was becoming light and vibrant again. I literally felt this within myself and noticed it as I began to handle situations in a different manner.

Like a plant that has been given light and water I started blooming into this beautiful woman. I studied the Word of God every day. Each moment I had to myself I'd dedicate that time to Him. I started to feel happy, healthy, and renewed. My mind started to see things from a different set of eyes. My spiritual eye was open. I was able to discern what was right and what was wrong not only in my life but in other peoples' lives around me.

That true communion with God allowed Him to start delivering me from evil. I no longer felt as if I belonged to this world or that this world even understood me. My life had new meaning a higher meaning and I understood what I needed to do. I felt blessed and encouraged. My obligation level to the Lord increased as our relationship blossomed into that of Father and daughter. I was able to grow in wisdom and knowledge of my true being.

When I bathed at night I found that I was relaxed and physically felt more open in terms of hearing

Him speak to me. After I'd bathe I would allow myself to take advantage of the quiet time I had and talk to Him. I would lie all of the days worries out before Him waiting for either an answer or His comfort.

In doing this I came to realization that watering the mind, body, and soul was extremely important in regards to our overall health. It had never dawned on me before that the element of water was so crucial to our very existence and not just because of consumption. When we bathe in warm or hot water our pores open up. When our pores open up it allows for our blood to circulate more efficiently, strengthening the cardiovascular system allowing the entire body to function as it should while your impurities are being flushed from your system. I personally have experienced quit a few breakthroughs when my body was in this state. The relaxation alone put my mind, body, and soul at ease.

I'd pull out my notebook and start to journal not just because I'm writer but because it was a great outlet for my emotions, thoughts, ideas, as well as documenting growth. The journaling experience pushed me to read more Scripture. The closer in relationship I got to the Lord the more Scripture began to make sense. I soon found myself pouring out my heart onto page after page of my notebook regarding the meaning of Scripture. With that understanding came His presence on a more frequent basis.

I learned that my issues stemmed from love or lack thereof. I had no clue as to what true love was. Me being like my mother, I had confused love with lust and sex. I had never felt unconditional love a day in my life. I say this not because no one had ever shown me compassion, care, or nurtured me. I say this because I had not known God. There were many years that I spent without this knowledge of Him. His love showers us with a feeling of comfort that cannot be explained and that can only be obtained through His Word and your own personal relationship. The only way to truly feel this overwhelming feeling of joy is through His Son Jesus Christ, who is the bread of life.

These intimate moments with our Father led me to this truth. I was determined to experience communion with God in a very special way. I mean I had been baptized at the age of 16, saved at 26, but my deliverance didn't start until I was 29 years old and that was a process in and of itself. The battle was not easy but mandatory and now I know the truth. Not my truth or the next person's truth but God's truth. As we proceed you will find the truth as well and start to experience life as God has prepared for you.

WEEK ONE

Ingredients

- Bible
- Notebook
- Pencil/Pen
- Drinking Water
- Bathing Water
- Time
- Commitment
- Faith
- Trust

It is very important for us to start this journey correctly. There are a few things I would like for you all to commit to doing during this first week of studying this book. It may seem like a lot but trust me His burden is light and the time will present itself to you.

- *Designate at least 30-40 minutes out of each day to pray, cleanse, study, and write. If you can devote more time please feel free to do so. If you are just starting out in your walk it's important to build your thirst for the Word. You do this by spending time with the Lord.*
- *Increase your intake of water in the Biblical sense and physically. We want to be fully nourished so that the roots of our new foundation are planted firmly. The element water that we drink not only opens us up spiritually to receive God, it also energizes our*

muscles, improves our brain function, mood, the beauty of our skin, and more.

Day 1 Journaling

Today I want you to think about your overall life. Sit back take time and really meditate on your life and all of its experiences. Now I want you to zone in on an issue that has been plaguing you from some time and has caused you to stress, depression, sadness, etc. Write about that experience today. Include your thoughts, feelings, and emotions about this ordeal. At the time how it made you feel and how it is affecting you today. At what time did you recognize this had become a negative force in your life?

Day 2 Journaling

Yesterday you wrote about an issue that has been plaguing you for some time now. Today I want you to take some time out to think about how you have responded to this experience or situation and how your responses have affected you in your life today. What was it inside of you that caused you to respond negatively in thought or actions to this particular issue? What is/was the right thing for you to do? Are there other ways or better ways you could have handled this adversity? Write about this in your journal.

Day 3 Journaling

Let's dig a little deeper today. Now that you know the issue that you are facing and have brought it to the forefront, are there any underlying issues that you feel needs to be addressed? Deep inside of your heart what do you feel this was all about in terms of you as an individual and your growth as a woman? Do you see where you could have or should have learned something about yourself in this situation?

Day 4 Journaling

When we talk about the Word of God and its' ability to nourish our minds, bodies, and souls was there an opportunity for you to display an act of faith in this area of your life? When your trust and belief in the Word of God is added into the equation what do you see about this situation? What do you know about the Holy Spirit that can comfort you in your moment of insecurity?

Day 5 Journaling

What do you think God was trying to convey to you in this particular situation? What was it that God wanted you to learn from this circumstance? Think long and hard of all the different lessons that could be taken from this situation. Even if the issue at hand was something that caused harm towards you and you were at no fault. How do you believe God could use you to fulfill a purpose that derived from experiencing this?

Day 6 Journaling

Take a few moments to meditate on the Peter 2:24. It talks about us being healed by the wounds Jesus Christ sustained when dying for our sins. Think about the wounds you have been living with each and every day speak this Scripture over you today. Look at yourself in the mirror and speak it until you believe it. Think long and hard about how being healed from this mental, physical, or spiritual ailment that has been hindering you will alter your life. Write down what you see for your future once you have overcome this obstacle.

Day 7 Journaling

Praise the Lord Hallelujah we have made it to the end of our very first week. After thinking about some very crucial experiences in your life and taking the time to put things into spiritual perspective how do you feel? Are you motivated and ready to begin this journey of healing and growth? Take some time to think of some other things that may be hindering you in your life. Do you see a common thread is there any one area of your life that God seems to be leading you to? Take some time to pray over yourself and speak healing. Write about the expectations you have for yourself in the weeks to come. Which promises of God would you like to see manifest in your life?

THE BREAD OF LIFE
(2)

Miracles of Life

"Mom, can I please stay home from school today?" My ten year old daughter pleaded with me that Tuesday morning. "I want to see the twins!" she exclaimed excitedly. I didn't want to keep her from school but what could it hurt? She didn't miss school often. After all she was coming to an ultrasound appointment to see the babies that were growing inside of me.

Although the father and I weren't together, I was still excited about being pregnant. They'd given me something new to look forward to. No matter how any of my babies were conceived they'd always been a blessing to me. Being designated by God to be a mother had to be the single most amazing gift He could have ever given me. I was the overseer, the main factor in bringing life physically into this world and that meant a lot to me.

I finally gave in to my daughter, telling her she could stay home from school to see the babies that morning. As we headed towards the state line we were becoming more anxious by the second. When we finally arrived at the facility I filled out the paperwork waiting for my name to be called. When the nurse opened the door to call me back, my daughter and I wasted no time following her down the hallway into a small room.

    I did as I was told in preparation for the procedure and waited for the nurse to start. She began to talk me through the process one step at a time. Placing the warm gel on my stomach she explained the procedure that would take place in detail. I already knew what was going to happen but none the less I listened to her with excitement and a huge smile spread across my face. She slowly ran the equipment over my stomach for what seemed like forever. My excitement gradually began to turn into panic as this uneasy feeling swept over me.

    I knew that something was terribly wrong. I waited for the sound of my babies heartbeats but there was nothing. I looked up at the monitor trying to see the dots that should have been bouncing around inside of me but all I saw was stillness. The nurse looked at me as I stared at her with pleading eyes. I could tell by her facial expression things weren't right. I closed my eyes as she began to speak.

    "I'm sorry honey I can't find any heartbeats. You're going to need to call your doctor now." I could see the sympathy plastered across her face as my heart sank down into my stomach. "If you'd like I can call them for you." She suggested. I wasn't trying to be rude but I couldn't respond. I was at a loss for words. Had she just told me that neither one of my babies had a heartbeat? Could she have been wrong?

    I declined her assistance in calling my doctor dialing my OBGYN on my own and leaving a message for them to call me back. I couldn't wait another second however so I rushed myself to the hospital. Surely they would be able to tell me something different. Maybe this woman was wrong. I mean the facility wasn't an actual "doctors" office anyway. There could be some type of error. I needed confirmation from a medical doctor.

I was still holding on to hope that this was all one big mistake and that my babies were fine. After my daughter and I spent several hours waiting for answers in a hospital room we were hit with the news. My babies were moles, both of them. They had started to form in my womb but the cells just continued to replicate themselves over and over like a cancer never forming a fetus.

It felt as if the entire world was crumbling around me. Breathing had become a task I was unfamiliar with as grief plagued my entire being. The pain of losing a child let alone two at the same time is something I can't even begin to explain. A child without parents is an orphan, a wife or husband who's lost their spouse is a widow or widower, but what is a mother who has lost her child? My mind was in a state of disbelief. I didn't know what to do with myself. So I wept.

Since my babies were still very much so inside of me the hospital referred me to my OBGYN to schedule a DNC. Three days later I was speaking with my doctor about the procedure which would take place the following week. For nine days I walked around with my deceased babies inside of me. And although they had never really technically formed into babies, I still had an overwhelming feeling of loss and grief.

When the day finally came for me to have the DNC I was filled with an unimaginable sorrow. I walked into the hospital lobby with my family beside me for support. I couldn't stop crying. My heart was so heavy, heavier than it had ever been. I shook and cried as I waited to be called back into the OR. I was heartbroken and couldn't help but wonder why? Why was this happening to me? I was losing two of my very own children simultaneously.

My heart beat a million beats per second as I waited in the lobby. When they called me back I followed the nurse on wobbly legs to the OR shaking and crying uncontrollably. After changing into the gown, getting my IV, and speaking with the doctor it was finally time to move forward. I remember being told to count backwards from 100 as the anesthesia flooded my veins. At 99 all was black.

When I finally woke up I literally felt empty. My eyes darted around the recovery room trying to register where I was. I'd hoped I was dreaming. It wasn't a dream though. This was real and it hurt. I noticed a nurse in the room standing beside me.

"Are my babies gone?" I asked as my entire being became engulfed in pain. She shook her head acknowledging what I'd already known. I clutched my stomach yelping out in pain. The nurse tried to console me the best she could but I couldn't be consoled. The hurt was too deep. In that moment I'd felt like I'd lost a very large piece of who I was.

In 2011 I found myself in the bathroom stall at work speechless. My hand shook as I stared down at the stick that dangled from it. I called out to my coworker who just so happened to be in the restroom at the same time as I. Reaching under the stall I asked her to tell me if I was reading the results correctly.

"Oh my God Keima, we're having a baby!" she

screamed excitedly as my heart began to pound out of my chest. I had so many different emotions running through me I didn't know rather to be happy or afraid. The loss of the twins had taken a lot out of me and I was truly afraid to try again. It was hard for me to be excited about being pregnant after what had taken place. A part of me however, longed to give birth to a healthy baby who I could love with all my mind, body, soul, and heart.

The day came when my faith was truly put to the test. I was at work when I started to spot blood. I began to go into emotional overdrive thinking about losing yet another child. My health insurance hadn't become effective yet, but I needed to see a doctor immediately. I left work heading straight towards the emergency room, alone. They conducted a multitude of tests including an ultrasound. For several hours I waited. Finally the doctor came in to see me. I could feel the energy her body emitted as she entered the room and I knew I was going to get bad news. I braced myself waiting for my results.

"I'm sorry," she started with a look of pity on her face. "It seems that you have a blighted ovum." I had no idea what a blighted ovum was but it couldn't have been good. She hadn't mentioned anything about the health of my baby and to say the least I was confused. I mean a blighted ovum sounded like a cyst or something that could cause complications in my pregnancy not termination. The next words that came out of her mouth were the same ones I'd heard another time before. "You're going to have to call your doctor to schedule a DNC." Tears began to roll down my cheeks it was too much to go through again. She walked over to me slowly kneeling down giving me a hug just before exiting the room.

I don't know how many times I read the discharge papers. I couldn't believe that this was happening to me again. Why? What had I done to deserve this? I researched what it meant to have a blighted ovum. It was a condition in which the sac had formed to carry the baby but nothing was actually growing inside of it. There was no fetal pole, nothing. It was just empty like I'd felt inside. Eventually my body would reject this "foreign object" and I'd have a great chance of miscarrying on my own.

I scheduled an appointment with my doctor for an ultrasound in which they told me that I still had a blighted ovum and that I should schedule a DNC. I didn't want to believe that, so I declined, and told them we needed to wait longer. I set up another ultrasound appointment for a few weeks later something in my heart was telling me it wasn't over. God didn't want me to give up in that moment.

The time came and my child's father accompanied me to the appointment for support. He had been my voice of reason and encouragement during that time acknowledging the fact that God didn't make mistakes and that we would deal with the issue together. When the tech began the ultrasound every muscle in my body immediately became limp as I smiled with tears of joy forming in my eyes. I looked over at my significant other and I could see his tears in his as well. There she was bouncing around inside of me like an Olympic Gymnast. Her heartbeat was strong and healthy it was a miracle! "They" said she didn't exist but there she was out of nothing, out of nowhere God had blessed us with this wonderful gift of life.

Our Lord is in the miracle making business and

it doesn't matter how big or small the situation, God will make whatever needs to happen, happen. In the book of John we learn about the miracles that Jesus performed. His very first miracle being making water into a wine at a wedding, the second was healing the dying son of an official. One miracle which seems almost meaningless and another that seems important are strategically placed one after another to show Gods exceptional grace and mercy to those who love Him.

Jesus made water into wine for a group of drunken men at a wedding as his very first miracle and healed a dying child as His second. That signifies that no matter where we are in life, no matter what we are doing, He will still work towards making our lives better. It doesn't matter how big or small the miracle, Jesus can handle it. He will see you through, if you just follow Him to the Father having faith in the goodness that God can and will do within your life. I didn't know how good God was until He gave me my miracle baby. She came from nothing and entered this world the largest of my four children and perfectly healthy.

I learned that there may be situations we experience in our lives where we feel as if we need God to perform a miracle in order for us to live. We may want results right then and there but the truth of the matter is that He knows just the right time to produce them. Even though I was not doing the right things when I became pregnant with the twins or Miriam, He blessed me anyway. I had lost two children at once but when the time was right I'd gained another. He showed me that He is the Bread of Life.

When I lost the twins I didn't pray to God one

time. Instead, I constantly asked the question why becoming angered. I threw temper tantrums blaming Him for my own misery. With Miriam things were different. Although I hadn't grown into a mature Christian woman I was on my way. When the doctors told me that my baby was not in my womb my faith grew instead of diminishing. I fell on my face and I prayed for a miracle, peace, and comfort because I had already experienced the pain of losing a child. I asked Him to be with me because I couldn't handle losing another baby. In that moment He saved us both.

It was at that time I realized how much I was loved by Him. I began to make small changes in my life. They weren't the biggest changes but it was progress. I was on the path to living a righteous life and was eager to learn. The road to redemption was bumpy but I was riding it. Wheels falling off and everything I refused to pull over. I had this overwhelming feeling to not stop. I learned that losing the twins wasn't about hurting me or the death of my babies. It was about my salvation and understanding of the life I had to live. Instead of saying I would die for my children I realized I had to live for them.

Those two experiences made me want to do right in all aspects of my life. It was imperative that I be a role model for them. I needed to be a woman that they could admire and never be ashamed of. I needed to be a woman who embraced who she was in Christ and despite her past found the courage to eat the "Bread of Life".

Keima A. Campbell

A Pricey Transgression

Change is never easy; however it is necessary when we make the choice to truly live. It is a process that at times causes a lot of pain and in some instances fear. In turning away from my sins I was forced to face my past transgressions head on and I will be the first to tell you at times I felt as if I was failing.

Some days proved to be harder than others. I'd asked myself on numerous occasions, how do I change or is changing even worth all of this suffering? I had been a certain way all of my life and now in my thirties I had decided it was time to become someone new. During those times of questioning I'd find myself drifting back to my past. The things I hated most about myself flooding the gates of my mind causing me to second guess myself.

At eighteen years old I knew it all. I was beautiful, young, and had my entire life ahead of me. I wanted to live life to the fullest and hit the ground sprinting through life at a very fast pace. I had been walking long enough. It was time for me to get out and explore everything the world had to offer me. All things were for the taking. I wanted that and then some.

What I wanted I got even if it meant selling my soul. The ad at the time felt like a Godsend. I needed money and according to the paper hanging from the bulletin board I could make plenty of it. How hard could it be? I was beautiful, I had a body a lot of women would kill for, I could dance, and I had a really good talk game. Why not get paid big bucks creating an illusion? I was ready to sell to whoever bought my lies.

Aside from the sweat, filth, and musk that filled the trailer my first call wasn't as tough as I'd expected it to be. The dim lighting gave me some added confidence and the older Caucasian man's calm demeanor and attentiveness gave me much needed comfort as well. The marijuana filled cigar and two shots of crown royal didn't hurt either.

When his time was up, he complimented me on my beauty, dancing skills, and presented me with "gifts" in addition to a hefty tip added to my hourly rate. He promised to become a regular and indeed he did calling the agency setting up a "date" once a week. It was guaranteed income. Word got around and soon I had a few regulars. The more calls I took the more I gave into the illusion that I was holding some unseen power over these men. As I made more money, my addiction to drugs, alcohol, and cigarettes increased.

I thought I was living the life. I was breezing through every single day stumbling without even realizing it. As I dove headfirst into the industry the darker my world became. Money had become my god and I was willing to do any and everything to get my hands on it. I had become the illusion I was creating for my clients. In reality I was their whore. My mind told me that who I really was didn't matter. What was between my legs would ensure I had everything I needed and more.

The day came when I was offered to take my "career" to another level. I had gradually begun to do more and more during those private parties, so when my newest client asked me if I was willing to do a few extra things I agreed. Dancing topless had turned into dancing nude. Dancing nude opened the door for touching and fondling. Touching and fondling bought me a first class ticket to performing sexual favors.

It didn't matter to me I had plans for that money. When I pulled into the parking lot of the office space my stomach became queasy. I shrugged it off as I counted the money I was going milk out of my new client in my head. As I glanced up at the building I saw a few people walking down the stairs which struck me as odd because it was pretty late at night. I told myself they were working late and I had nothing to worry about.

I pulled some items out of my bag and began prepping for my date. From the corner of my eye I noticed something moving so I directed my attention towards the driver side window. A heavyset African American man was making his way to the car. When he reached me he pressed his police badge up against the window.

It felt as if all the energy poured out of me, as my head dropped shaking from side to side. My heart was pounding so hard I could hear it in my ears and feel it in my throat. I knew that I was going jail. I considered for a brief moment putting the car in drive and taking off but that thought quickly disappeared as I thought of all the ways that could go wrong.

I hit the locks on the door without even looking up, expecting to be dragged out of the car, cuffed, and hauled off to the county jail. Instead, he proceeded to the passenger side of the car nestling himself into the seat next to me. I sat there quietly with my hands gripping the steering wheel so tight that the whites of my knuckles could be seen even in the dim light. I couldn't say a word.

"You're a lot prettier than I thought you'd be," he said breaking the silence. His words seemed cold and calculating. I remained quiet trying to keep my composure. "You know," he started, "They always let the white girls go and lock up all the sistas. So I'm going to do something for you tonight. I'm going to let you go too." He said touching my leg. "But before I can let you leave, I need you to do something for me." He stated calmly. He tried to pretend as if he were doing me a favor but I knew better. I waited for the devastating blow to be delivered.

He didn't say another word as he slid his hand up my dress allowing his fingers to invade my sacred place. He removed his hand from between my legs examining his fingers and commenting on what was my innermost sacred treasure. I wanted to run away. I didn't want things to go down like I knew they would but what could I do? Who could I tell? It would be his word against mine and who was going to believe a prostitute? My heart almost stopped when I heard the sound of his pants unzip. "Come here," is what he said before he did everything he wanted to do to me in that car.

Now some might say I asked for it. Maybe I did. However, my consent had been revoked once his motives changed. I consider it rape. As an officer of the law I should have been taken to jail. Instead, he chose to violate me.

When he was finished he pulled out his business card telling me how much fun he'd had and for me to call him sometimes. I sat there too shaky to move so he threw the card on the passenger seat before closing the door. I sat there for what seemed like hours before I cranked up the car and rode out of the parking lot. I was in a daze. I know what I had planned to do but what happened caused me to rethink my situation, reconsider the turn my life had taken.

Becoming lightheaded I pulled over into the parking lot of an all night diner. I was hot I needed some air. I could smell the stench of the sin that had taken place just moments before and I couldn't handle it. As soon as I opened the door my body thrust forward and I emptied the contents of my stomach for what seemed like the entire year. I threw up until nothing was left and still I dry heaved for what seemed like an eternity. My chest hurt, my head hurt, my entire body was in physical pain. Tears rolled effortlessly down my face, two, three, maybe four of them at a time. Tears of pain, sorrow, disdain, and shame.

It was that night that I began to believe that my beauty was a curse and that I was a worthless piece of trash. Although that was the last night I took a private call I didn't leave that lifestyle completely alone. I was addicted to certain aspects of that life. I was addicted to hurt and pain. I deserved to feel that way is what I told myself.

For many years I battled with that memory. It made sense for the enemy to present this experience to me as often as he did when I had cautiously made the decision to live for the Lord. It wasn't until I started making this change that I began to understand the significance of the things I'd went through in life. It was so easy before to question God saying, "How could you let this happen to me?" But with age and experience came wisdom. It wasn't God who put me in the situations that I'd found myself in time after time. It was my own sowing that reaped the consequences I had to face. Had it not been for God miraculously placing His hand on me, I wouldn't be here to tell my story.

I had to learn that the Bread of Life is Jesus. He is nourishment to our souls just like the food we eat is nourishment to our physical bodies. Without Jesus we become weak, frail, and fragile. We are unable to sustain life because there is no life in us. We continue to die a slow and painful death much like that of someone suffering from malnutrition. That was what I had been lacking for all those years, the Bread.

That was why the enemy saw fit to bring memories such as those I expressed to you back to my remembrance. The need for me to starve my soul was imperative for him to steal it. Just as we work out to get our bodies toned and healthy I had to begin working out my soul. I started to become cautious of what I watched, listened to, and spoke. I allowed my ears to hear the gospel of Jesus Christ. I took in as much Living Water as I could to eliminate waste, cleanse and purify that which was dehydrating my soul.

Jesus Paid It All

As I started to become conscious of that which was unhealthy for me and turned away from it I felt a strength I had never known before overcome me. I was purging the sin from my soul so that I could become clean again. In order to turn from sin I had to keep God's commandments. These commandments being the starting point of my journey but most definitely not the end.
- No Other Gods, only Me.

- No carved gods of any size, shape, or form of anything whatever, whether of things that fly or walk or swim. Don't bow down to them and don't serve them because I am God, your God, and I'm a most jealous God, punishing the children for any sins their parents pass on to them to the third, and yes, even to the fourth generation of those who hate me. But I'm unswervingly loyal to the thousands who love me and keep my commandments.
- No using the name of God, your God, in curses or silly banter; God won't put up with the irreverent use of His name.
- Observe the Sabbath day, to keep it holy. Work six days and do everything you need to do. But the seventh day is a Sabbath to God, your God. Don't do any work-not you, nor your son, nor your daughter, nor your servant, nor your maid, nor your animals, not even the foreign guest visiting in your town. For in six days God made Heaven, Earth, and sea, and everything in them; he rested on the seventh day. Therefore God blessed the Sabbath day; he set it apart as a holy day.
- Honor your father and mother so that you'll live a long time in the land that God, your God, is giving you.
- No murder.
- No adultery.
- No stealing.
- No lies about your neighbor.
- No lusting after your neighbor's house—or wife or servant or maid or ox or donkey. Don't set your heart on anything that is your neighbors.

Being aware of what was expected of me through

His law helped me in my journey towards enlightenment. Knowing these commandments increased Gods Love towards me and opened the door for Him to make Himself known to me. I was able to see Him and the plan He had for my life more clearly. I knew that I no longer had to allow myself to be repeatedly stripped of my dignity. God who had been there all along was able to give me the peace and happiness I had longed for all of my life. I didn't need to swim in murky waters that bound me.

There was still one problem however. I wondered why was it that although I felt better and my burdens were being lifted from me, there was this feeling that it was more to this lifestyle. I wasn't sure how to get to it. So I continued to study the Word planting seeds into my brain. The more I read, the more God's peace settled inside of me, preparing me for what was going to be revealed to me next.

I came across this Scripture; **John 6:32-35 (ESV) "Jesus then said to them, 'Truly, truly, I say to you, it was not Moses who gave you the bread from heaven, but my Father gives you the true bread from heaven. For the bread of God is he who comes down from heaven and gives life to the world.' They said to him, 'Sir, give us this bread always.' Jesus said to them, 'I am the bread of life; whoever comes to me shall not hunger, and whoever, believes in me shall never thirst.'"**

When I ate the Bread of Life which is Scripture I became aware of Our Lord and Savior Jesus Christ. He is the Word of God made into flesh. Who better to hunger and thirst for? The One who knows us better than we know ourselves, our Lord and personal a happy life, to obtain peace beyond all understanding, and know unconditional love. I was no longer suffering from spiritual malnutrition and on my death bed clinging for life. I was more alive than ever.

I ate this bread everyday and every night. It filled me up until I felt as if I was overflowing with joy. It was spilling out of me into my children, my mother, whoever I came in contact with. It was flowing like a calm stream. For the first time in my life I truly felt beautiful. I wasn't insecure nor was I searching for something I would never obtain. I just was and Scripture was right, I didn't yearn to be fed anymore.

Week Two

Ingredients

- Bible
- Notebook
- Pencil/Pen
- Fruits/Vegetables
- Bathing Water
- Drinking Water
- Time
- Commitment
- Faith
- Trust

What we eat is of great importance to our overall health and wellbeing. A great tip for maintaining the body and being healthy is to become mobile. Eat more frequently and try to snack on things like fruits, vegetables, and nuts to satisfy cravings for things that are unhealthy for your bodies. Make sure to snack every two hours in between meals with a large glass of water to keep yourself full and energized.

The only way to experience what the Bread of Life has to offer is to accept Jesus Christ as your Lord and personal Savior. You can do that by saying this:

Lord God, I come to you in the name of Jesus. I acknowledge to You that I am a sinner and I am sorry for committing sins against you and for the life that I chose to live. I pray Father God for your forgiveness. You said Lord God in, Romans 10:9 that if we confess to You and believe in our hearts that You raised Jesus from the dead, we shall be saved. I am confessing to you right now Lord God. I know Father God that Jesus died for my sins and was raised again from the dead. I accept Him into my heart and into my life as my Lord and personal savior. I declare according to Your Holy Word, Grace, and Mercy that I am saved. In Jesus' Holy Name, Amen.

Let's focus on nourishing our spiritual bodies:

Day 1 Journaling

When you think about the pain that Jesus endured in order to fulfill the purpose God had over his life what emotions and thoughts come to your mind? How do you believe the pain and suffering that you yourself have endured in your life prepared you to fulfill the destiny that God has placed upon your own life? In answering these questions write down how you feel about this.

Day 2 Journaling

What is it that you desire most for your life at this very moment? What do you feel you need to be fed in order to fill that void that you have in this area of your life? Why do you believe you desire this for your life and how do you believe this need can be fulfilled?

Day 3 Journaling

Considering all that you have suffered and sacrificed during your lifetime can you think of a way that you can serve God through what you have been through? Is there a way that your story can bring fulfillment to someone else's life that may be going through an exact same situation that you have overcome in the past? What is it about this situation or circumstance that has you hanging in the same spot unable to move forward and turn this moment adversity into a moment of success?

Day 4 Journaling

At the beginning of this week we pledged to God that we accepted Jesus Christ as our Lord and personal Savior in doing that we let go of ourselves and fully became His. What does it mean to you to no longer belong to yourself but to belong to God? ***Colossians 1:16 (ESV) "For by Him all things were created, in heaven and on earth, visible and invisible, whether thrones or dominions or rulers or authorities—all thing were created through Him and for Him."*** Consider this Scripture and what does this tell you about yourself and who you are?

Day 5 Journaling

Write out a list of anything that you consider negative that is currently invading your life at this time. What types of thoughts or behaviors feed these negative things? What causes you to become unglued or give in to the negativity that surrounds these issues? How can you take responsibility for what is happening around you and focus on a positive outcome that can be brought about from this same situation?

Day 6 Journaling

Take a few moments to ponder on the following scenario. You are a friend of God. The two of you are walking in a meadow filled with a beautiful array of flowers as the warm sun basks down onto your skin. You smile taking in the smells of the spring air. Butterflies are floating in the air and you feel a sense of peace. You glance back noticing a storm is approaching from behind. It's a big one you look around but there is nowhere to seek shelter. You forgot that you were with God. His presence you have totally forgotten about as you panic in the moment. What do you think God would say to you once you realized that He was there with you the entire time? Is there anything you think that He would do in the hour of darkness that was approaching waiting to attack you while you were not fully aware? In recognizing God standing beside you in that moment of fear or despair your outlook on the situation would change?

Day 7 Journaling

Pray to Our Lord God. Explain to Him what it is that you think you need in your life at this time. What is it that you will have accomplished by obtaining what you believe you need at this time? If you do not have this need met how will it affect your life? Is this need better assessed as a want or it crucial to your survival and your quality of living? Is there anything that you are holding on to that feels bigger or more powerful than you and the God inside of you? In what ways can Jesus' walk help you in assessing your own walk and being accepting of the trials and tribulations you have to endure to reach what God has in store for you?

FOOD FOR THOUGHT
(3)

Falsely Abused

The abuse was almost constant. He'd always have something to say to tear me down. It had become such a big part of my life that I began to believe every word said against me. Even during those times when he'd wanted to act like a loving husband all I could really focus on was the fact he wasn't. I'd question why he was even with me.

I'd given my life to him. Bearing his children and saying I do was only a small part. I believed in being an encouraging and loyal wife, so I stuck around even when it meant sacrificing my own joy and happiness. Although he'd taken every tragic experience I'd shared with him and formed a weapon against my self esteem, spirit, and self worth, I thought having him around was better than being alone.

We'd been fighting and then making up for years. Each incident leaving me a little more broken but with hope that one day we'd be able to truly love one another. At the rate we were going however the truth was becoming painfully clear. Things weren't getting better. In fact that notion was farther away than I could have ever imagined. With each altercation my dream of having a meaningful marriage faded.

I'm not sure why we were fighting but our words spilled into the atmosphere like venom from a deadly snake. I knew where it was leading and as much as I didn't want to take it there, I couldn't walk away. If I tried he would follow me barking in my ear, poking, pushing, until he got what he wanted. So I stood my ground waiting for the fighting to begin. Truth was I was so tired of fighting and arguing. My heart was heavy and I could feel my soul drowning in the agony of domestic violence.

The first blow interrupted that brief moment of revelation that filled my soul. My carnal instincts kicked in and I began to fight back. Fists were flying landing wherever they could. For some reason this time felt different. This time I felt as if I were fighting for my life. After several heavy exchanges I felt myself being lifted into the air and slammed to the ground.

The impact was so powerful it caused me to become slightly disoriented. I tried to move but he had me pinned against the floor. I couldn't do much of anything except lie there and wait for whatever was next. I looked up searching his eyes for any sort of humanity and compassion towards me but there was none. What stared back at me were empty eyes. They were eyes that didn't have a soul behind them, evil in its purest form. My heart began to beat against my chest so hard that I could hear it in my ears. The pounding sent a vibration throughout my entire body.

I stared intently into his eyes hoping to see a glimmer of the man I'd tried so hard to love. There was nothing there. For the first time I noticed the statue he held high above his head. To this very day I remember feeling the rage seeping from his entire being. I thought to myself, *this is it. This is the end of my life.* My daughters were going to witness me being murdered by their father in our own home. They would grow up orphans with no mother or father and with the memory of that one dreadful day.

I'd heard about people who had near death experiences having their lives flash before their eyes. I didn't necessarily have the opportunity of being shown the highlights of my own life but I saw my daughters living without me. I lay underneath my husband in this daydream for what seemed like an eternity. Everything, even time seemed to have stood still as I pondered deeply what my life had become. I had a deep sense of calmness fall over me. Although I could still hear my heart beating the fear was gone.

My feeling was once again interrupted this time not by the blow I was expecting to the face but by my daughter who was five at the time screaming at the top of her lungs. At first I wasn't sure what was going on. Then I noticed her little body behind her father tugging at his shirt and hitting him in his back. She was screaming, "Get off my mommy!" My baby at five years old had come to save my life.

I should have been saving her. I mean after all I was her mother. But none the less that one act snapped her father out of his trance. The life came back into his eyes as he pulled himself off of me and walked away. I lay there breathing as my little girl ran to my side hugging and crying over me. I felt ashamed. I was the parent she should have never been subjected to our ignorance.

In that moment it was very clear that what we had between each other was over. We could not be together any longer. If we continued to stay together someone was going to get hurt very badly or worse lose their lives. I slowly found my strength and with the help of my five year old I made my way to their bedroom on wobbly legs.

I began to panic when I couldn't find my oldest daughter. My heart broke when I opened up their closet door to find her curled into the fetal position crying. This was what domestic violence had done to our children. I wasn't the only one battered they were too.

I could feel death lingering and I refused to take any more chances. Our relationship was toxic and dangerous. I had been completely striped of everything I had once known myself to be. Now I was just there going through the motions. I made one of the most valuable decisions of my life. I chose to leave.

I got some clothes and made my way to my grandparents' home with my babies. It wasn't long before he started to snoop around my grandparent's home trying to get me to come back. As he always did, he'd promise never to hit me again, and apologized saying that things would get better.

Then he would switch the issue up to be about him and the pain from his childhood. The abandonment, the hurt of growing up without a mother and father, or the fact that his mother was addicted to drugs and spent most of his life in prison haunted him. My face had become those things. I was the poster child for all his pain. I was who had to pay for every single thing everyone else did wrong to him.

I stood my ground. I never fully went back although I kept things cordial between us. On February 15th 2007 he put his hands on me for the last time. When it was safe, I called my mother and asked her to come get the girls and me. She'd said that if she left work to come get us and I went back that she would never come again. I understood and was prepared to finally leave after seven years of abuse.

What should have taken an hour was reduced to 30 minutes and the sight of my mothers' face brought instant relief to my soul. If I couldn't count on anyone I knew I could always count on her to be there. We drove to the elementary school to pick up my daughters.

I will never forget the confused look on my five year olds face when she saw us standing outside of her classroom. She asked why we were there. I told her we were moving with her grandma. She let out a heart wrenching cry as she dropped to her knees in the hallway with tears flowing freely down her little cheeks. It was a cry of relief. I know because I'd felt it too. It was time to get away from the chaos. Start a new life, a better life, a life of peace.

We made it to my mom's house without incident and even the mere smell was calming. The air there was light and welcoming. For the first time in a long while I was able to truly exhale. I lied on her couch running my fingers through my hair. Although I was relieved to be there I didn't know what I should do first. How do you start your life over?

I noticed big clumps of hair entangled in my fingers. I walked into the bathroom for privacy. For the first time in a long time I saw myself in the mirror. I looked horrible. I had dark rings around my eyes, my skin was blotchy, and my hair was falling out. Being in an abusive marriage had taken it's' toll on me. Not only had I felt battered I looked battered as well.

Demonic Thought Processes

How do you start a new life? Life has many ups and downs. At times we may experience so many downs we lose sight and forget to look up. The trials and tribulations that sometimes hit us from all directions can seem unbearable.

Our minds hold on to memories of all the bad that has happened and store them for future reference. We take our mistakes and experiences and allow them to become who we are. So it's no longer what we did or what someone else did or said to us, those things now define us. We tell ourselves we aren't meant to have peace of mind and happiness.

We begin to doubt everything we once believed in until we are caught up in this tsunami of emotion and have no idea what is real and what's fake. And because bad things sometimes happen the enemy slips in through the tiny crack of doubt and turns our world upside down. We are tricked into a mental state of hell.

With leaving my violence filled marriage a whole other set of issues I'd have to face emerged. I was forced to live with myself. During this time of trying to get back to the "old me" I realized a lot about who I thought I was and what I really thought of myself.

I was guilty is what I told myself on a regular basis. I should have never been born. Here I was barging into my mothers' life when she was only 19 years old. She didn't plan on getting pregnant but she kept me. I'd turned her, an innocent girl into an instant mother, trying to figure out who she was and raise a daughter at the same time.

I was guilty for allowing my daughters to live in a household plagued with domestic violence. I plead guilty to selling my body for a profit. I was guilty for not breaking the cycle of becoming a teenage mother. I was guilty of lying, cheating, stealing, and hate. My reality told me there was nothing I was not guilty of.

I was not a child of God because I didn't know how to be one. I didn't want to look God in His face because I was ashamed. Or maybe it was because I wasn't sure if He really existed. Had He been real I would have never had to learn such painful life lessons. He would have never allowed me to get caught up in the mess that I found myself caught up in on so many occasions.

I had to fight my entire life but for what? Why had He allowed me to have even been born? I could only ask why. I was so angry if God had come down and given me the answer Himself I wouldn't have been able to receive it. It wasn't because I didn't really want the answer. It was because my mind was closed to the truth. My thoughts kept me from understanding the way God needed to communicate with me. So I remained stagnated in the same rut I had found myself in time and time again.

Because of this I started to become angry and bitter about everything and towards everyone. I began to isolate myself from my friends and family emotionally. The isolation I thought I needed opened the door for the captivity of my mind. I was being held captive by a set of invisible chains. Chains that pulled me back each and every time I tried to move forward.

These chains would snatch me around to face the left and remember that my father had abandoned me and didn't love me. They would pull me up to my feet just to snatch me down by the neck causing me to remember how many times I had fallen prey at the hands of someone I trusted. They'd spread my legs so that could I remember how many times I'd degraded myself just to feel temporarily worthy of someone's attention.

These chains kept me from eating. They held me in that dark place called despair so that I could never move forward. They bound me in a bottomless pit of sorrow that I had no idea how to get out of. They kept me running back to what I thought was the only thing I knew. Even when the chains were broken I stood there afraid to move. I was afraid of being happy and living in peace. I realized I was addicted to pain. The same pain that was killing me from the inside out had become my crutch. It had become the only thing in this world that I truly trusted and believed in.

The Beginning of the End

A person knows when they are fed up with a situation. My anger, resentment, and pain had started to take just as much of a toll on my psyche and body than the beatings from my ex-husband had. I had finally reached a point where I was sick and tired of being sick and tired. I needed to find a better way. This didn't just happen on my own accord however. It took one of the most tragic incidents in my life to push me towards the light.

I stood in between the two men calming them down attempting to become the voice of reason. These were my friends, my brothers; this couldn't go down like this. I didn't want to witness what was transpiring right before my eyes. I walked slowly towards my friend speaking to him in a calm and soothing manner. The gun he held in his hand slowly began to drop down to his side. But not before it went off piercing through my stomach.

Everyone disbursed and suddenly I was all alone. I could see the police and ambulance in the distance.

They were at the nightclub responding to a shots fired phone call. I tried to call for help but I was too weak for them to hear me. I attempted to run towards them but it seemed every step I took increased the distance between me and help.

I was dying I'd felt it deep in my spirit. I pulled out my cell phone in one last attempt to get an ambulance. If only I could get up the hill. My phone wouldn't dial 911 my fingers couldn't hit the numbers correctly. I wasn't afraid just warm. I called my mother and told her to tell my kids I loved them before closing my eyes.

I woke up sweating looking around filled with overwhelming sorrow and fear. I'd never had a dream about being shot and dying. I was shaking uncontrollably. My home didn't feel right, I didn't feel right. I felt as if death was lingering around me.

I tried to go back to sleep but I couldn't. For the next couple months I lived in constant fear. I would drive to work and all of a sudden I would have this overwhelming feeling that I was going to die. It was to the point that I would burst out in tears not knowing if the moment consisted of my last seconds here on this earth. I couldn't explain why I felt that way. I didn't want to tell anyone about it because I thought my family would think I was insane.

Then the day came. June 13, 2009 one of the most sorrowful days of my entire life. I had fallen asleep on my couch and was awakened by the ringing of my cell phone. It was my mother. She spoke to me in a calm manner, "Booder got shot," she stated calmly.

I couldn't believe what I'd heard. Did she just say Booder was shot? She had to have the wrong information because Booder had been the calm one out of all the boys. He never got into altercations and always kept a level head. He stayed smiling, laughing, and joking. I sat up in disbelief waiting to hear that he was okay. When my mother confirmed that he was alright he was in the hospital I felt relieved. At the time I didn't know the details of what happened but as the eldest of all the grandchildren I knew I had to make it to him right away.

I asked my mom if she was ready to go and she responded with no hesitation as she got her things together rushing to my house so we could drive the hour it took to get back home to Topeka. My heart wasn't heavy I knew that he would be alright. We had spoken with our family and they told us that he was okay and was in surgery. My aunt his mother even suggested we stay at home but we couldn't. We needed to be there.

The surgery took forever and the lighthearted feeling I had when we first got there slowly began to fade as time progressed. I needed him to hurry up, get out of surgery, so I could tease him about interrupting my beauty sleep. But, when he came out of surgery I couldn't joke with him. He wasn't conscious, he had tubes everywhere, his eyes slightly open, and he wasn't breathing on his own. I took my turn in the ICU sitting outside of his room watching him rest.

My heart was heavy. I didn't like seeing him like that. The sight literally sucked the breath away from me. There he was tubes everywhere, his stomach rising with each second fighting for his life. I started thinking about all the memories we shared. How I was so jealous when he was born. After being an only child for almost 8 years and here he came taking all of the attention away from me. That jealousy however, turned into unconditional love.

I worked two jobs and would spend my entire check taking all of the kids bowling, skating, out to eat, to the movies, shopping, whatever it was they wanted to do we did it all in one day. I sat there laughing about the time I thought he needed a haircut so I'd taken a pair of scissors and cut it for him. There were patches everywhere. By far that was the worst haircut he'd ever had. The smile that began to creep across my face quickly disappeared as I noticed the commotion that was taking place inside his room.

The nurses had called for the doctor, who acted as if he didn't really care about what was happening with my brother. He muttered something under his breath and walked away. The nurses looked at each other unsure of what to do next. My heart ached and I knew he would not be ok. One of the nurses asked me to leave. I did as I was told and we were soon informed that he was going back into surgery they hadn't stopped the internal bleeding.

After several more hours of surgery the surgeon called my aunt back into a small room to discuss his condition. She was told that we had to prepare ourselves to tell him goodbye. It was impossible for them to stop the bleeding and that at 20 years old Booder would be returning to heaven. The pain was unbearable, his death seemed more like a scene from a movie than the reality that was my life at that moment.

Booder was my brother, my baby, I had taken care of him, nurtured him like he was my very own at one point in time. His life couldn't end. He needed to see his 21st birthday; he needed to watch his two children grow into upstanding adults. Even though he was almost eight years younger than I he'd taught me how to be unselfish. All of these emotions bombarded me as I started to become lightheaded. The next thing I knew, I was waking up in the ER.

Attending his funeral was one of the hardest things I've ever had to do. Until this day I have yet to go to his gravesite. I can be honest with myself and you in this moment. I have not been able to come to terms with his death. To visit that gravesite to me would be to give up on the fact that I will see him again. My take on death may or may not be healthy but when it is time to come to terms with this, I trust God will steer me in the right direction of understanding and enlightenment.

As if life wasn't already complicated enough the irony of Booder's' death is that it brought me life. After losing someone whom I held so dear to my heart I started to search for the answers to all of my whys. I knew that there was only one place I would know the truth and that was to find God.

I'd heard once or twice that God's Word was Living and Active. The word active means working, operative by definition and living means active, alert, and alive, so when I began to speak His Word aloud over my life I started to see my life changing. People say that change takes time but my life was changing instantly.

It wasn't because of what was happening all around me. Truth is nothing had changed in that aspect. The world was still the same. His Word was literally purging the demonic thought processes from my mind and giving me hope, peace, and love. Everything that was clouding my mind was replaced with a light that shined so bright people began to notice.

The weight of worry had literally been lifted from my entire being. My mind was expanding and I was able to see the endless possibilities of every circumstance and situation that showed itself against me in a different light. I started to see this adversity as a way for God to show His Mighty Power in my life. I recognized none of those things that happened to me were even about me. In fact they were about God and all that He is capable of doing. I was still standing.

I was still strong despite the things I'd seen and done. God had a place for me. There was a reason behind my being. There was even more reason regarding all the adversity I had faced. ***Romans 8:28 (ESV) "And we know that for those who love God all things work for good, for those who are called according to His purpose."***

Scripture does not say some things it says **all** things. That Scripture alone convicted me. It let me know that I in fact was not the bad decisions I made. I was indeed a child of God because even in my darkest hour when I questioned Him and threw my temper tantrums trying to figure out why this or that, I still loved Him. I still knew I needed Him.

In that moment of enlightenment it became very clear that I was ready for restoration of my true being. My life had not been one big failure it was a huge success. I had figured out the secret to life. If I focused on the teachings of Jesus Christ everything would be clear. I'd be intelligent beyond any amount of years and possess the ability to discern what was real and what was "real fake".

Since Christ is in charge of the entire universe and belongs to God and God is in charge of everything even beyond space and time, I too belonged to God and Christ. If my life is revolving around God's Son the headmaster of the universe then by adapting to His lifestyle my life is made easier. I received comfort in knowing that. The fear and sadness that used to grip me and bring me into depression had ceased. Replacing it was His kindness, grace, and love.

It wasn't merely just the words; kindness, grace, and love. It was the actual feeling that flowed through my entire body that let me know that what I was feeling was absolutely beyond a shadow of a doubt, real. It was the Love Experience that got me. I didn't even care about the why something happened to me anymore. I was more concerned with how I could give Him more glory, how I could do something else to make Him proud of me for being exactly who He made me to be.

That was my peace. It had been there all along. I didn't need to go searching for it. The more I read about His Word, the easier it was for me to keep my eyes, ears, and mind focused on Him. When I did this consistently, I started to think like God. His love and compassion overpowered me and I was not the "old me" I was looking for.

I was a new and improved model. Top of the line nothing else like it in this world. That gave me the confidence I always pretended to have. The cracked door of doubt was sealed up airtight and nothing was coming in or going out.

Even with this new life I found there was still this and that going on here and there. As strange as it may sound it seemed as if more people became angry with me, attempted to persecute me, and push me to my limits. But God's Will, took over me and I could not be moved. I refused to go backwards. So I allowed myself to remain focused on the prize. The prize being, Him.

Week Three

Ingredients
- Bible
- Notebook
- Pencil/Pen
- Fruits/Vegetables
- Bathing Water
- Drinking Water
- Time
- Commitment
- Faith
- Trust

Have you ever thought about why you did something? Every decision that we make, every action that we take starts with a thought. We just do not do things just because we see the opportunity to do them. We do them because something in our mind triggers us to turn a thought into action. In order to act holy and to be Godly we must think holy and Godly. It is important to purge all negativity from our thoughts in order to manifest a positive outcome over our lives. As long as we love Our Father with every fiber of our being beginning with our mind all things good will be added to us.

This week will probably be the most crucial week of this newfound life that we are living. I say this because renewing our minds is such a tedious task to do. Although we spend one week on doing so in this book cleansing and renewing our mind is a lifetime process. As we continue our journey we will find something different that we must work on each and every day. It is almost like peeling the layers of an onion. There will be a lot of crying along the way. But tears are cleansing for the soul. His Grace, Mercy, and Love are the things that give us peace, hope and life here on this earth.

We will continue drinking from the fountain of eternal life as we allow the Spirit of God to pour Itself into us. We will remain eating from the Tree of Everlasting Life by consuming the Word of God, meditating and marinating on what He has said.

We will also speak these things into existence. We will speak His promises over our lives so that our minds will begin to transform into powerful vessels of wisdom, love, and understanding. The peace that we gain from the renewal of our minds is what sets us up to be prepared to do God's Divine Will in our lives. In exchange for this obedience we will prosper in all areas of our lives. The reward for walking a righteous path is beyond our physical ability to comprehend.

Each day we will participate in an exercise as well as journal about a specific scripture. The purpose of these exercises is to assist us in figuring out some of the things that are hindering our minds and blocking us from receiving our blessings. We have to actively unclog our minds of meaningless things and fill it with the things that matter, holy things.

<u>*Day 1 Journaling*</u>

Answer this question: Who am I? When describing yourself think of as many words as you can and put them into two separate columns one consisting of what you consider negative and the other things that are positive. In addition to defining who you see yourself as write down what happiness means to you and make a separate column of what are some things that make you happy and some that do not. (Keep this list in a safe place to reference back to later to see your growth).

1 John 3:1-3 (MSG) "What marvelous love the Father has extended to us! Just look at it—we're called children of God! That's who we really are. But that's also why the world doesn't recognize us or take us seriously, because it has no idea who he is or what he's up to. But friends, that's exactly who we are: children of God. And that's only the beginning. Who knows show we'll end up! What we know is that when Christ is openly revealed, we'll see him—and in seeing him, become like him. All of us who look forward to his coming stay ready, with glistening purity of Jesus' life as a model for our own."

How does this Scripture affect how you think about yourself? Do you see yourself differently now that you know who God says you are? Why or why not?

Day 2 Journaling

Have you ever been labeled by other people or even by yourself? What have you been called in your lifetime that has stuck with you even until now? This can be positive or negative labels. Is this truly how you view yourself? What characteristics do you have that would cause people to portray you to be this way? Do you recognize any events that have happened in your life that have caused you to develop these characteristics? How do you feel about those events and the way they have shaped your life?

Day 3 Journaling

As women a lot of times we can act out on emotion. We tend to be more sensitive to situations and circumstances becoming angered, hurt, saddened, stressed, etc. based off of what we see in the physical. The frustration of a lot of things we experience and have to go through as women can cause us to be resentful and bitter. When we try to communicate sometimes our emotions will spill out into one big whirlpool. They drown us and who we're communicating with. We have to learn as women to have self-control; otherwise we will get caught up in the moment making hasty decisions. This week let's really focus on our emotions. Was there a situation that caused you to become emotional? What happened, what were you thinking and doing the moment before you became emotional? Who were you with? Why do you think that situation caused you to react that way? Did the person or people you were with recognize the emotions you were feeling? What does this say about you and why? How do you think the others who were with you or around you felt about your behavior? Keep a chart of these things so you are able to recognize your triggers in the future.

Day 4 Journaling

Do you have any thinking patterns that could be hindering your spiritual growth? Are you constantly comparing yourself, or beating yourself up about things that happened in the past? Do you find yourself beating yourself up about someone else's situation? Blaming yourself about what has happened in their lives? Have you found yourself blowing things out of proportion or making assumptions about what others are thinking about you?

Day 5 Journaling

What are the things you have done or the traits that you feel you have that you cannot and do not accept? What could you do in your life to right those "wrongs" and make yourself more acceptable to yourself? Think about how you deal with conflict. Choose a specific conflict and list how you felt, what you did, and how you think you could have handled the situation better. What could the outcome have been if you handled it that way? Now list some things you can do in the future that can help you to do what is acceptable in God's sight.

Being acceptable to God makes us acceptable to ourselves. If we are filled with God and honoring Him in all of our thoughts and actions we start a new life. Journal about the importance of starting a new life. What do you hope to obtain by accepting responsibility for your actions and making a conscious change in the decisions that you are making?

Day 6 Journaling

Look in the mirror what do you see? Be honest with yourself, are you truly happy with who you are not just on the outside but the inside as well? If you were to remove all of your makeup would you still find yourself beautiful? Are you searching outside of yourself for happiness? Make a list of things that make you happy. Take some time to think long and hard, if you did not have these things, if you were unable to attain these things how would you feel about yourself? Is "stuff" what makes you happy or is the substance of yourself what makes you happy?

Journal ways in which you can allow yourself to let go of everything and put all of your trust in God. If we are too busy searching outside of ourselves for happiness we miss out on the blessings that God has for us. His gifts are far greater than anything we could ever imagine in our own minds. How can you pray for God to truly move in your life without being preoccupied with everything the "world" has to offer?

Day 7 Journaling

Discover what brings you peace. Ask yourself what do you need to be at peace with? What do you need to let go of? Pray a prayer to God specifically for deliverance from everything that is making you suffer and taking away your peace of mind. Rebuke any feelings of fear, discouragement, doubt, lust, arrogance, etc. in the name of Jesus, thanking God and believing that He is able and it is done.

Are you abandoning the way of Jesus Christ? Or do you choose to live in perfect peace so that you too will have conquered the world through Christ?

PRIMER
(4)

Long Lost Love

At 22 years old the time had finally come. I'd waited to see him all my life. I couldn't believe he had actually called and wanted to meet with me. I was given extra assurance when I found out he only lived fifteen minutes away from my home. God had to have planned this out for me.

I imagined that we had unknowingly passed one another in the grocery store at one point in time. Maybe we'd exchanged a warm smile or even a simple head nod at a stoplight once before. I had high hopes that once we locked eyes with one another we'd have an immediate connection and we'd fall in love just like that. He would see so much of himself inside of me that he'd have no choice but to love me.

It surely didn't happen that way. We met up at a fast food restaurant near his home. When I walked in I knew immediately who he was and instead of being greeted with a warm hug and a hello a grimace fell upon his face as if it pained him to look at me. I felt as if he were disgusted by what he saw. None the less I swallowed the lump that had formed in my throat, smiled that smile I was accustomed to plastering across my face and took a seat across from him.

The first words he said to me were, "You look just like your mother." The statement lacked any type of emotion. Although my mother is very beautiful his statement was anything but a compliment. The venom that seemed to seep in his words tugged at my soul knocking the very life from me. I pretended as if I hadn't noticed and began to introduce him to my children, his grandchildren.

Despite the awkwardness of our meeting we found out we had a lot in common. We even laughed a little bit. When the moment of truth had come and we decided to touch base on his absence in my life he didn't spare my feelings. His answer was simple he had no excuse other than he didn't want to be involved with my mother, even if it meant not knowing me.

I didn't quite know how to react to that statement. I knew my mother could be difficult at times but he'd chosen to be involved enough with her to have unprotected sex with her on numerous occasions. But that was neither here nor there. The good thing is that we intended to keep in contact with one another. That was enough for me. I was finally going to get the closure I'd needed.

The next of couple weeks were like a fairy tale. Although my father and I didn't see each other anymore after that initial meeting we spoke on the phone every single day. He told me it was pleasurable to speak with me. He said I was like a breath of fresh air. I cannot even begin to explain how such small words made me feel about myself.

My entire life I had waited to be validated by my father and that time had finally come. The feelings I had for my dad grew deeper in that moment. However, as with most of our lives things aren't always what they seem. Life doesn't usually play out the way we hope or pray.

So when my mom called me with the news I was beside myself. She had been the person to locate my father and give him my contact information. I was grateful for the initiative she took in helping me. In the process of her contacting my father however she also contacted his wife. She was not as open to the fact that I wanted to have a relationship with him.

Until this day I am not 100% sure of all the words that were spoken between my mother and his wife but I can only imagine. For some reason she thought it to be odd that after 22 years I wanted to have a relationship with my father. She wasn't okay with that. As opposed to creating drama in my life or my fathers, I thought it best to just back away. I truly felt like my father would straighten things out.

I would have loved to meet his wife and was looking forward to having another female role model other than my mother and all the wonderful women on her side of the family. My intentions were never to cause any problems between the two of them. I stopped calling my dad and he also stopped calling me. It was five long years before I would ever see his face or hear his voice again.

It was a bright and sunny Sunday morning and my mother and I had driven from Kansas City to Topeka to spend some time with my grandparents. My Granny was excited we'd be spending the entire day with her at church. Needless to say we were just as excited. There's something about my grandmother that makes people want to put a smile on her face.

Although I was filled with joy there was something brewing in the atmosphere. I had an unexpected surprise waiting for me that day. Unbeknownst to me my father was actually a preacher. He was a guest speaker, at my grandparent's home church on that particular Sunday. When I first laid eyes on him I got butterflies in my stomach. I hadn't known that he represented a church in Kansas City. Then again I suppose we never made it that far for him to tell me. Maybe he felt embarrassed or thought that having me showing up in his life would tarnish his reputation as a man of God, either way the reality was his absence had caused me to question my self-worth all my life.

Even then, seeing him made me long for a relationship with him. At 27 years old I still wanted my daddy in my life. I held on to that hope that he would see me and be wowed by how I had grown since he'd last laid eyes on me. We'd talk and start all over again. Again that hope was shattered when we met with him outside of the church.

He spoke to me very briefly, barely acknowledging me to be truthful. In five seconds flat he was in my mothers' face, flirting, complimenting her on her beauty, and even going as far as asking her for her cell phone number, as his wife sat in the pews of the church waiting for him to come back inside. To say I was floored by his actions would be an understatement. I felt disgusted but not just with him even so with the church in general.

I grew a deep seeded hate for him and an even deeper hate for myself. His rejection was one of the hardest pills I've ever had to swallow. Sure there have been times where I've had to experience extreme physical, emotional, and mental pain but what I felt in that moment with him surpassed it all. This pain was so draining that the only thing I was left with was a feeling of emptiness.

The wound was too deep for a band aid this time. I needed it to be packed with love. I needed to understand what it was I needed to do about this situation that continued to hurt me, to haunt me for as long as I could remember. I couldn't make him want to be a part of my life. So now what? What was I supposed to do?

Prepared For A Purpose

The answer to my what was now simply this.... Move forward! God had already prepared me for the life that I was living. It was time to stop making decisions based upon what I was lacking and to make some based upon all that I had access to.

God doesn't put anymore onto us than we can handle. He makes the path clear for us. We just have to stop allowing someone else's sins against us to affect the outcome of our own lives. While I was asking God why, I should have been asking Him why not?

Had God spared me the presence of this man to keep me from reliving that feeling I had on that Sunday afternoon? The mere thought of his rejection for the third time in my life turned the joy I had into great grief. If my father had made a choice to stick around how often would he have disappeared?

Was my true Father saving me from the constant pain that a man I didn't even know kept subjecting me to? Could this feeling of abandonment lead me into my life purpose? How on earth could I give God the glory behind such circumstances?

Here I was abandoned by my own father while I was still in the womb. I met him 22 years later and he abandoned me again. Five years after that at age 27 he wrote me off on the steps of a church as if we didn't share the same bloodline. To add insult to injury he was referred to as a "man of God." Those are the facts. The situation to this day in 2014 has not changed.

But God said in, **Proverbs 16:4 (ESV) "The Lord has made everything for its purpose, even the wicked for the day of trouble."** It's very important to start with this Scripture. It says that the Lord has made EVERYTHNG for its purpose. That includes me. It was time to forget the circumstance and focus on the "everything" or in my case the "someone" at hand.

I'd spent many years questioning myself and never getting the answers I wanted because I thought they were based off something I was missing. A father. The truth of the matter was He was there with me all along. I had the Father of all fathers by my side and hadn't even thought to consider Him as being who I could turn to and find what I lacked.

This path although not a path I would have chosen for myself prepared me for the life God had set for me from the start. There is nothing that can or will take away from God's plans. What He says will come to pass is exactly what will come to pass.

I always had what I'd been praying for, but never realized it. I asked for a Father and **Psalm 68:5 (ESV) says, "Father of the fatherless and protector of widows is God in His holy habitation."** I couldn't have asked for a better Father. The Creator of all things considered me His daughter! I have a Daddy who is Love and who has never and will never leave me nor forsake me. I have a Father who sacrificed His Perfect Son who was without sin so that I could be saved from my own sins.

According to statistics 1/3 of American children grow up without their fathers. That's a total of approximately 15 million children in a single parent home ran by their mothers. At one point in time I was one of those children. That number increases every year. I questioned myself, how many of those children have felt the way I felt in regards to being fatherless? How many of those children go out into the streets searching for that love that they truly believe they are missing from an absentee parent?

God didn't allow me to experience this life for nothing. There are millions of boys and girls just like me who struggle with this truth about their lives. There are millions of children who need to know that not knowing their father and in some cases their mothers or both is not their problem. They aren't the problem. They aren't the issue. They were made to be someone great. The only way for them to understand who they truly are, is to understand where they truly came from.

So where did we come from? Is it our parents and our ancestors that shape our future? Or is it God? **Psalm 139:13-16 (NIV) "¹³ For you created my inmost being; you knit me together in my mother's womb.¹⁴ I praise you because I am fearfully and wonderfully made; your works are wonderful, I know that full well.¹⁵ My frame was not hidden from you when I was made in the secret place, when I was woven together in the depths of the earth.¹⁶ Your eyes saw my unformed body; all the days ordained for me were written in your book before one of them came to be."**

God knew us even before our beginning started here on earth. Our lives were written. So although things look bad or they feel bad they're always going exactly as planned. Not only are our lives recorded, but there's a plan of action that will allow us to remain at peace with everything we are faced with.

Because we live in a world filled with ungodly things it is inevitable that we will be faced with many trials and tribulations. These are the tests of life. These tests create our testimonies. And it is our testimonies that provide hope for others who are having trouble along the way.

Despite how we feel about our lives there is purpose. The hell we have been through was necessary in order to show that heaven is real. The pain we've experienced in life was to only show us the true power of healing. The endless possibilities derived from God's Love are like primer to our souls. It is what smoothes out every bumpy road we have traveled down. On our way back up to His Grace and Mercy that has fixed the cracks and potholes creating a smooth ride even when our vehicle feels as if it is on the verge of breaking down.

You don't have to beat yourself up about your past, present, or future. Just continue to look up to the heavens. This way you will find comfort and understanding in your purpose. God has prepared you for a very happy ending. Your hurt has not been in vain.

With life experience comes knowledge, and with knowledge comes belief, belief brings us into faithfulness, and faithfulness opens us up for God's Favor and Blessings. When you begin to question rather you are coming or going know there is light at the end of the tunnel. When everything seems....hard. Trust that what God has for you is for you. What you are experiencing is hard labor. God is in the process of birthing something great out of you.

Be patient and be brave because He is always with you. We are strong because He is strong. The adversity we face is necessary for our growth. A flower cannot grow without the storm. The winds may be strong and lightening may come crashing down but believe that the God who made you is all powerful. He is your shelter at all times.

He Brought It To My Remembrance

The day had started off like any other Friday with me blasting my music as I gave my apartment a thorough cleaning. Out of nowhere I was flooded with a million thoughts. I felt an overwhelming sense of urgency that was so strong it almost took my breath away. My soul was crying out to me for change. I needed to take a long hard look at myself and the way I lived my life. Don't get me wrong I wasn't doing anything "bad" but my Spirit was telling me I wasn't doing much good either.

Then life's pain rushed to the forefront of my very being smacking me in the middle of my face. I sat down for a few moments buried in my thoughts, feeling grieved. I'd tuned everything and everyone out around me. It was just I and my past in a face off. My past staring me down, and me refusing to look away from it. I noticed my future passing me by as I struggled with the things of my past. It was drifting further and further away.

In that moment I knew that there were so many things that had to be put to an end. I couldn't just bury these things alive. I had to let them die and stop feeding them. They needed to be starved to death. The life of not only me but my children depended on it.

I couldn't stand back being timid and afraid, asking questions like why? There was no why, the real question was how can I show others God's light through that darkness? How was God in the mix the entire time I was wounded by others and even myself? Was He there?

Those are some of the same questions that had haunted me my entire life but I finally had the answer. Yes! He was there! Some things I didn't have to go through but He allowed me to because He had a big plan for my life. None of what I had been through was even about me. There was no vendetta against me like I'd always thought.

I was made to do Kingdom Work. Of all the hell I had been through, God was not going to make it all in vain. Like Jesus was risen from the dead so was I. The rape, the abandonment, the drugs, the abuse, the reckless lifestyle I had been accustomed to was all a part of a bigger plan. It was God's plan.

It had been so long since I had been in the Word of God but at that moment I thought about the story of Moses. His mother hid him for three months to save his life and then she had to give him up. He was put in a basket and sent down the Nile River by his sister. They didn't know what was going to happen to him. What if the basket sank and he drowned? What if crocodiles came and ate him alive? What if no one ever found him and he starved dying alone in the River? Their faith in God was strong they trusted Moses would be ok. He was okay. He was adopted by the Egyptians and raised as the Egyptian Princesses son.

How does an adopted child feel when they think about their parents? Do they believe they were abandoned for valid reasons? Are they truly understanding of the circumstances behind their parents' decisions? Or do they wallow in their own grief becoming insecure with themselves questioning their very existence? Was that insecurity what caused Moses to stutter? Was that insecurity the reasoning which allowed him to scrutinize himself when God Himself spoke to him from the burning bush?

It was not by chance however, that Pharaoh's daughter found Moses in that river. Nor was it by chance that Moses was taken in and raised living a very privileged lifestyle. Neither was it by chance that God had strategically placed him in a position of authority although he was a Hebrew so that he could later lead God's Children out of captivity. All these things God prepared.

He even made Pharaoh's heart hardened so that He could show His children that no matter how powerful a man is, no matter what the circumstances are, no matter how long you have been in a predicament, He is God and He is more than a conqueror. He will place you in a position of total freedom.

Let's even consider Job. After he'd become sick and gotten weary, he went back to Our Father recognizing that it was all preparation for God's elaborate plan. What happened next? His children who seemed to cause him much grief with their partying and sinful behaviors were replaced with obedient children who were beautiful on the inside and out. His riches were increased even more than before. His health was restored and he was no longer lying on his deathbed.

Although he had experienced great tragedy Job came out better off than he ever was. He saw God work miracles in his life. His prayers were answered in every aspect of his life. So hold on my sisters your breakthrough is yet to come. Accept God's Will for your life and watch how your entire world will begin to change for the better.

When you hear that voice that comes from deep within listen carefully. When you least expect it God will reveal to you where you need to go. He will convince you deep within your heart that the changes you make are necessary. There is no rhyme or reason to when you will know it'll just come so be prepared. Life is all about preparation. Expect the unexpected and nothing in life will surprise you.

Week Four

Ingredients
- Bible
- Notebook
- Pencil/Pen
- Fruits/Vegetables
- Bathing Water
- Drinking Water
- Time
- Commitment
- Faith
- Trust

Primer is an essential product in achieving optimal coverage and overall look when putting on makeup. Primer is what reduces the size of pores and creates a smooth surface ensuring long lasting wear of the finished product.

Day 1 Journaling

Make a list of three things that have happened in your life that caused you to ask God why? Sit and ponder on those situations and think of the negative aspects of those circumstances and write them down. Now on the same sheet of paper list some positive things that have or could have come out of that specific situation. How you can use that experience to show God's light to someone else?

Day 2 Journaling

Write a prayer about a specific trial or tribulation God has delivered you from.

Romans 12:12 (MSG) "Be alert servants of the Master, cheerfully expectant. Don't quit in hard times; pray all the harder."

Journal what being an alert servant means to you. Take time out to really sit and ponder the meaning of being an alert servant to the Master. What is this scripture saying about God in hard times? Why do you think it says to be cheerfully expectant?

Day 3 Journaling

Write in your journal your thoughts concerning patience and tempered virtue. How do you think this is obtained through trials and tribulations? Can you name a time that you experienced a trial and the outcome was this? What was your attitude when going through the motions? Do you think your outlook on the situation could have changed it?

Day 4 Journaling

Write in your journal how we benefit from living in harmony with that which surrounds us? What does being harmonious have to do with being prepared for the lives we live according to God's plan?

Day 5 Journaling

Have you ever found yourself using the trials and tribulations you've experienced as a crutch to not move forward or to come into who you know you can be? Is there anything you need to be honest with yourself about? Where you are wrong or flawed make a commitment to expose those things and write out a plan of action that changes these things about you and gives you the integrity you need to be a woman of great stature.

__Day 6 Journaling__

Even through all your mistakes, hurt, and pain think about why you are a good person and why you believe God has called you by name to share His light.

__Day 7 Journaling__

James 1:12 (MSG) "Anyone who meets a testing challenge head-on and manages to stick it out is mighty fortunate. For such persons loyally in love with God, the reward is life and more life."

What does the reward of life and more life suggest in this Scripture? How does sticking it out through the good and bad effect relationships in general? Now think about being loyal to God and sticking with Him through the good and bad. What fortune do you see yourself inheriting by staying committed to His Kingdom?

CONCEALER
(5)

Uncertainly Certain

I sat in the small room in the basement of the church wringing my hands and looking at the clock. I wore a white robe that covered a pair of lounging pants and a t-shirt. I knew this was something I had to do. I mean getting baptized was the only way to get to heaven right?

My mind wandered back to my childhood. *"Mommy who is God?" I asked. I'd heard about Him before but I wanted to know more about this mysterious being.*

"He is our Father." she said smiling. "We have to pray to Him every night and not sin or else we'll go to hell." She added continuing to smile.

What was she smiling for? I may not have known God at the time but I knew where and what hell was. I surely didn't want to burn there. I didn't know what sinning was either. I wondered how I could not sin. "What is sinning?" I asked unsure of if I really wanted to know the answer or not.

"Sinning is when you do bad things like lie, cheat, steal...." I am sure she went down a whole list of things that were sins but all I heard were the first three. I was trapped in a whirlwind of fear. I had lied! I lied about not breaking something. I didn't want to get into trouble so I said I didn't do it! I had cheated in a game of kickball a time or two. I had even cheated during hide go seek so I would know where everyone was at! I hated losing!

I was panicking in my own mind until I heard, "But your sins can be washed away if you are baptized." I gave her a peculiar look and she went on to explain what baptism was. "I was baptized when I was a little girl," she said smiling bigger than she normally did. Even though she was happy I wasn't! I didn't go to church! I couldn't remember a time that I had ever stepped foot in a church. How was I ever going to get baptized?

My heart was pounding. I didn't know what to do. I swallowed the lump in my throat believing that there would be another catch. This was a lot of bad information for a small girl who wasn't baptized. I truly believed I was going to hell. Maybe it was the fear that crippled me into silence but I couldn't say another word. I kept quiet as my mother tucked me into bed with a goodnight prayer.

"Now I lay me down to sleep. I pray the Lord my soul to keep. If I should die before I wake. I pray the Lord my soul to take. Amen."

I stared at my mother waiting for her to say something else but she didn't! She just kissed me *goodnight. I knew if I died before I woke up I was going to hell because I wasn't baptized! I don't remember if she stayed in the bedroom with me that night until I fell asleep or not but at some point during the night I was awakened by the fear of dying. I cried that night and many nights after that for one reason only. Fear of going to hell.*

I snapped out of my daydream ready and prepared to make the biggest decision of my life. I was getting baptized just like Jesus. The couple of months that I'd spent going to church had been just what the doctor ordered. I was feeling great.

I felt anxious as I stepped into the small pool of water. I closed my eyes as the preacher spoke and dipped me into the water. When I came back up I felt new. I was clean. God was finally pleased with me and I thought that everything would be alright from that day forward. On my 16th birthday I gave my life to the Lord. I was ready to allow Him to pull me into safety. However, that brand new feeling of lightness soon began to fade and I couldn't figure out why. At some point I'd returned back to my old ways.

My quest for Truth and Love had been short lived because I had no idea what the quest actually consisted of. I didn't know the true reasoning behind being baptized. I was missing large chunks from my puzzle. That's when the enemy slipped in. I started to become doubtful that what I'd done was even the right thing to do. Why did it matter that I was baptized? It hadn't helped me. I was still doing the same things I'd always done.

Who Am I?

For many years I wondered who I was and how I could live a purposeful life. Did God truly have a purpose for me? In order to really know where I was going, I had to first figure out who I was intended to be.

When we think of knowing someone the first thing that comes to mind is that persons' name. Then we consider the things that person does, what their personality is like, and how they interact with others. How often than not however, is the way a person portrays themselves to be just an act? How often is it that we find ourselves playing a part in a movie about us while we're playing the role of someone else?

That was me for a very long time. I was exactly who everyone said I was. I was beautiful, had attitude, charisma, sexy, and a lot of spunk. My confidence allowed me to choose any boy I wanted. I was the chick that had good looks, a good head on her shoulders, and was going somewhere in life.

This is what a lot of people thought of me, but the truth was I was far from any of those things. On the outside I had a hard exterior. I didn't have a care in the world. I was confident, beautiful, and full of life. But on the inside I was dying. I experienced constant turmoil. In reality I was the opposite of anything anyone had ever believed me to be.

I didn't know whether I was coming or going. I wasn't sure of anything. So many people placed me on a level I had no clue of how to get to. I didn't feel half as confident in myself as the people on the outside looking in felt about me. I was being pulled by both arms in two opposite directions.

I wanted to be someone that everyone could like and love. At least that was how I felt one day. The next I didn't care who liked me, who was my friend, or even who I'd wronged. Life was all about me and what made me feel good for the moment. Everything and everyone else didn't matter. As long as I was happy and the world spun in my direction life was good.

At least that's what I told myself. The truth of the matter was simple. After every pain I caused someone else I felt ten times as bad. Every wrong decision I made became a big part of who I was. I myself was the wrong decision. I was confused. I had nowhere to turn because I had no one to talk to. I didn't trust anyone. Not even my closest friends knew about the pain I harbored inside. They too believed that I was happy with myself.

They thought I was strong but I was a weak link. I was hanging on to life by a single thread. Pretending to be everything I wasn't because I didn't know what I was. The truth was hidden from me. It was hidden because of my sin. It was hidden because the enemy didn't want me to know who I truly was.

If I knew who I was then I would know that I was more than the name Keima. I wasn't just a fatherless child. Neither was I made to fulfill a man's sexual appetite. How could I find out how to be the "real me" without feeling ashamed and embarrassed? I couldn't so I depended on other things to help me cope with living the lie.

Addicted

I smoked my very first cigarette at the age of 13. I didn't do it for any other reason but to try to be cool. I felt the need to set myself apart from the other little girls my age. I wanted to be a trendsetter. I forced myself to like the taste. I pushed myself to inhale the smoke into my lungs and blow it out for anyone in the vicinity to reap the consequences of inhaling secondhand smoke.

I didn't stop there though. Less than one year later I had become addicted to smoking marijuana. It wasn't just a temporary puff here and there. I was getting high every single day. At times skipping school for sex and drugs was mandatory and necessary for me to even function.

Still by the time I was in the 12th grade not only was I addicted to cigarettes, sex, and marijuana but alcohol had become a major part of my life as well. I would steal my mother's liquor she'd kept hidden under the sink every day before school. I just needed that buzz to be able to deal with my life.

When I became an adult it was nothing for me to pop an ecstasy pill or molly for "fun". At one point I'd pop a pill just to get through the day. The drugs and alcohol helped me to cope. It helped me to deal with my pain. I'd forget about my troubles and live in the moment. I would justify my behavior by telling myself, *"You only live once so live it up."* But once the high came down and everyone around me was gone, there I was, back at square one.

I was alone, hurting, questioning myself once again. None of those things were healing me. They were like a temporary fix to a problem that was boiling out of control. Eventually the fix had become a part of the problem as well. You see they were tearing my body down. The cigarettes were putting my children and me at risk of developing cancer. The marijuana was killing my brain cells threatening the most important organ in my body. My brain. It was the only organ that could put me back on the right track. The alcohol was jeopardizing the function of my liver, kidneys, and even altering my train of thought. My addiction to sex was putting me at risk of contracting sexually transmitted diseases, becoming pregnant, or worse dying.

I was consistently playing Russian Roulette with my life. For twenty years I battled with an addictive personality. By 33 however, I had managed to stop doing drugs and rarely drank alcohol. However the cigarettes still had a stronghold on me. As many times as I'd quit, I'd always go back. If something stressful presented itself in my life I'd light up.

Twenty years of smoking and I couldn't stop. I quit smoking weed, popping pills, I didn't really drink alcohol other than special occasions, but the cigarettes, I couldn't shake. It didn't matter what the studies said about second hand smoke for my children I continued to indulge. When I did try to stop, I'd go through these bouts of sickness. I'd experience uncontrollable coughing that forced a brownish black mucous out of my body. My chest would hurt so bad I could hardly breathe. My attitude during those times was horrible. I was anxious and temperamental yelling at my children for no reason at all.

I'd break down after a day or two rushing to the store to get my fix. After the first puff it was like every muscle in my body would relax. I was immediately calm again. My body would get this tingly feeling and I was "happy" again. Best of all the bouts of coughing would completely cease. I believed they were the answer to all my problems. They were the only way my soul could be put at ease. Tobacco had become my god.

Exposure to the Truth

John 10:10 (GWT) "A thief comes to steal, kill, and destroy. But I came so that my sheep will have life and so that they will have everything they need."

The enemy does not want to see us living the life that God intended for us to live. Instead he wants to steal our joy, kill our spirit, and destroy our future. If we don't believe there are brighter days ahead of us. Days where we can smile, laugh, live and enjoy our lives what use is there to strive for a better future?

We lose sight of ourselves, our hope disappears. Without that hope we have nothing. But notice in the Scripture Jesus says, "But I came so that my sheep will have life and so that they will have everything they need." He is assuring us that if we follow His way we will not be lacking anywhere. We won't be missing anything that is needed to survive this life. We can live peacefully, joyfully, and be comforted by the fact that all of our needs will be met.

Think about your life. If you have ever had a time where you were struggling with any situation, didn't it feel as if you were lacking not what you wanted but what you needed? Jesus says that He will make sure we don't need for anything. The Scripture doesn't say that He will only do this for a select few. It says He will provide for His sheep.

Who are His sheep? We are! Those of us who believe in Him and love Him belong to Him. No matter what we have done in our lives, what we've seen, or how long it took for us to recognize Him, the truth is He's ready and willing to make our lives better than we could ever imagine.

What the enemy tries to do is keep us focused on things that don't matter so that we lose sight of the fact that in reality we have nothing to worry about. Everything that we need can be obtained by simply opening our mouths to confess our sins and change our ways. Following and focusing on good and not bad in order to find the blessing in everything around us.

We don't need drugs, alcohol, or other people to take away our problems and pain. We need Jesus! His way is the only way to overcome the adversity that sometimes presents itself in our lives. Anything or anyone other than Him that we place the power of our lives with is an idol. We are not to worship false idols.

In finding truth we are no longer comforted by the lies of the enemy. We learn the undisputed truth about this thing called life. What is the undisputed truth? **Romans 5:8 (ESV) "But God shows His love for us in that while we were still sinners, Christ died for us."** So let's really break this Scripture down my beloved sisters. God shows His Love for us even while we are still sinners. Have you ever questioned how you were still here? Have you ever taken the time to sit back and reflect on your darkest moments in life? How did you make it out alive?

I'd ask myself those questions all the time. Going into the homes of strange men sometimes multiple men alone with no one knowing where I was at or who I was with was dangerous. There were a multitude of things that could have happened to me that I can't even bring myself to speak into the atmosphere.

I reminisce about the company I've kept. I wanted to be loved so bad that I would sit in a house full of guns and drugs just to be in the presence of who I thought was my true love. I would sleep at night with someone I knew was violent towards others just to feel "love". His actions could have brought me a lot of physical harm and even death.

Then the unthinkable happened. He was snatched away from me. Locked up in a jail cell because of the activities he was involved in. I felt like the breath had been taken away from me. I thought I was being punished. I felt like I didn't deserve love because of this situation. That was the story of my life. I'd finally found love and it was taken away from me. I wasn't meant to be happy.

The truth of the matter was this. God loved me more than I even loved myself which is why He removed me from every single dangerous situation or person I'd allowed in my life. I could have been kidnapped and killed. I could have been raped over and over again contracted HIV and AIDS and died. But God showed His Love although I acted out in ignorance. Although I believed every single word the devil had told me, God kept showing me the truth through His Love even when I was too blind to see it.

He never changes His mind about us. He waits to meet us exactly where we're at. The enemy tries his best to make us believe that our lives are meaningless and that we are just as worthless as our meaningless lives. But we have a Friend in God who will encourage us and help us to see what is real and what is an illusion.

There is no greater act of love than to sacrifice your own child to show others just how much you love them. There is no greater act that God could have performed than to place Himself in the flesh so that He could feel our human pain so that we could be delivered from every single form of evilness that plagues this earth.

Our lives are no less than those whom we consider are doing better in the "living" category than we are. We are all blessed to live from the moment we were formed in our mother's womb. We are all molded in such a way that our lives will make huge impacts on the lives of others. God's path will never hinder us only enhance us to be greater than we could have ever thought of being.

This life isn't even about us. It's about Him. The secret of living is to learn to grow in truth, love, grace, and mercy.

What does God's Truth do for us? ***John 8:32 (MSG) "Then Jesus turned to the Jews who had claims to believe in Him. 'If you stuck with this, living out what I tell you, you are My disciples for sure. Then you will experience for yourselves the truth, and the truth will free you."***

How does the truth free you? When we make a vow to change our live it seems like everything we have been taught turns out to be a lie. When God began to change my life I felt as if the truth was hurting me more than it was freeing me

Walls seemed to be crashing down all around me. I didn't realize it then but I was no longer being boxed it. I was indeed being freed from the bondage of lies that had become the barrier of my being. It wasn't the truth that was hurting me. It was the lie that covered the truth that had put me in so much pain. The truth had always been there like a calming pond offering me safety amidst an inferno of burning flames.

From the Truth which was not my truth, his, hers, or the others truth but God's Truth I was able to learn the true meaning of Love. God was Love and with His Love came the grace and mercy I thought only "special" people received. This could only mean one thing. We were all special to Him.

We are to know who we are and Whom we belong to. And in knowing this we expose the enemy for what he truly is, a deceiver. Once we recognize this in him based off the ungodly decisions we have made in our lives we are able to move forward and get to know ourselves better. We realize the connection we have to one another. We feel the love and compassion for each other. We are able to do what we were sent here to do.

By learning that I was a child of the Most High God I was heavily convicted that I had the power to do anything. If God was a part of me then how could I fail? If the Spirit of the Lord dwelled with all of His believers then I was connected. I was the sister of millions of amazing people from all walks of life, all financial and social statuses, and that meant I had the appropriate resources to change my entire life around. I also had the opportunity to help change theirs.

How To Find Yourself

In every Scripture concerning water it was symbolic of eternal life or freedom. I found that although water from baptism will only get you so far, the Holy Spirit is what catapults you into who you were made to be.

Holy Spirit? What is the Holy Spirit? ***John 14:26 (MSG) "The Friend, The Holy Spirit whom the Father will send at my request, will make everything plain to you. He will remind you of all things I have told you."***

Remind me of all the things He had told me? Why hadn't I known this all along? I had to let myself go and allow the Holy Spirit to fill me so that I could have access to the knowledge that was given to me before I was formed in my mother's womb. It was the Holy Spirit, the baptism with fire that would show me the true meaning of my being. God's way and His Divine Will for my life had finally been revealed.

When Jesus was baptized it wasn't for his own salvation it was so that He could show us the necessary steps to gain salvation through Him. God told Jesus He was pleased by the pledge He'd made when He got baptized. It symbolized His readiness and willingness to do God's Divine Will while here on earth.

The representation of the baptism was to show that if we follow the path of righteousness through Jesus Christ by being baptized and filled with the Holy Spirit we will be able to walk in the Word of

God. We also obtain eternal life, will be raised from the dead on judgment day, and awakened from our current zombie like state of thinking. Our spiritual eye will open and we'll be able to walk in the Spirit.

A lot of times we are breathing, moving, thinking, etc. but all of our thoughts and actions are dead. When I say dead I do mean that in the literal sense. It is important that we do things, we say things, and think things that bring forth life. Life is only obtained through allowing God to do His will through us.

Our Heavenly Father sent us the Son when He blessed us with Jesus Christ. That is why we call him our Savior. God knows that we are born with a sinful nature and sin separates us from God. When we are separated from God we are unable to see clearly. Our thinking, judgment and sight become foggy. So without the Word in the flesh for us to follow behind we would have no example to mimic.

We'd be unaware of how to become closer to God. Jesus was a teacher and teachers lead by example. He was God our Father sent down from Heaven to earth in order to direct us. Parents' guide us in the right path, they show us love, they nurture and care for us despite our shortcomings. God is the parent of all parents and He makes no mistakes. He knows all, sees all, and can do all, even fix us when we are broken. Who better to take on the sins of the world than He? He sacrificed Himself as the Son for our safety.

Our baptism is about more than pleasing God however. We are pledging to complete His Divine

Will. Each and every one of us was made for a Divine purpose. The water opens our spiritual eye to the endless possibilities of what God has for us according to Scripture. No Father wants his children to live in their own personal hell. It is tormenting to live a hellish lifestyle. We all benefit from having the gates of Heaven open to us and obtaining quality time with our Heavenly Father.

In addition to our baptism it is crucial that we seek His presence through His Word, prayer, meditation, and submission to Him entirely. Water not only provides us with eternal life but with freedom from all the things that keep us in bondage. ***Exodus 14:21-22 (MSG) "Then Moses stretched out his hand over the sea and God, with a terrific east wind all night long, made the sea go back. He made the sea dry ground. The sea waters split. The Israelites walked through the sea on dry ground with the waters a wall to the right and to the left."***

God helped Moses lead the children of Israel to freedom. The chains of enslavement were broken and God parted the waters for their escape. But the most gracious and glorious thing about the parting of the water is that the land was made dry so they couldn't get stuck.

I recall speaking to a Vietnam Veteran on the telephone one day at work. He was one of the sweetest elders I've ever spoken to. He began to chronicle his experiences in Vietnam. His story was so vivid I could see exactly what he had experienced in my very own mind.

I had to keep myself from becoming emotional because I had a job to do. When reading this passage in the Scripture it brought me back to what he called, being stuck in the muck. The platoon would trudge slowly through the muddy swamps of Vietnam as their feet would get stuck in the sticky marsh. One of their greatest prayers was that they wouldn't get ambushed, captured, and or killed while in the "wilderness". The process was so tedious that several years later many of them developed bad cases of arthritis.

But God..... In freeing His children, not only gave Moses the power to move the waters, He dried the land beneath their feet so that they could escape easily. He provided an escape route and ensured that no matter what it looked like, no matter how many people were after them that they would not get stuck nor taken back to that place of captivity. He does that for all His children. Hallelujah! We are safe with our Father.

God gives us strength to overcome every obstacle that gets in our way. He accepts us because He knows who we truly are and not what our environments or circumstances pushed us towards believing we are. When we act out against the general order of what God has prepared for us that is where confusion sets in. However, we must know that Our God is not a God of confusion.

We believe that WE can fix things. We may have graduated college, landed a great job, met a million celebrities and had relations with them, bought a $1200 pair of shoes but what do we feel like on the inside?

We hide behind our "stuff" and "people" we place on high pedestals. We lose ourselves allowing things outside of our true being to define who we are. We are concealing every great thing that God made in us. We expose our bodies in an effort to hide the beauty we can't find inside of ourselves. As women we fail to see that our beauty is beyond what is shown in our hips, bust, behinds, facial features, hair and nails. Our true beauty supersedes the clothes that hang from our bodies, the diamonds that dangle from our ears, necks, and wrists, the heels that adorn our feet.

Have you ever taken time out of your day to just ponder on what your life means to you? Really think. If you have everything materialistic that you could ever imagine in the end what has it done for your soul? I am not telling you that you can't or should not have nice things. What I am challenging you to do is to think about the value you place on those things. Find what is truly important to you and your spiritual wellbeing.

For those who do not have excess of anything I challenge you to ask yourselves are you placing too much emphasis on what you are lacking? Is what you're lack affecting your ability to gain in any area of your life? Sometimes we put a blindfold on ourselves concealing what is directly in front of us and inside of us.

How long will you allow yourself to miss out? I had allowed myself to miss all that God had for me for 29 years. Even when I had gotten saved, I still hadn't been delivered from the evil that was within me because I myself was unable to recognize the God in me. All things holy were still a mystery for a very long time.

Dying to me was the only way to truly know who I was. I had to allow Christ to live through me. Every decision I made, every word I spoke, I asked myself, "Is this how Jesus would handle the situation?" That simple task is what no longer makes us our own but His. So now the light that was concealed from us through the darkness of our sin is revealed. God conceals us with a veil that is bright so that we don't just appear righteous, WE ARE RIGHTEOUS.

We carry a set of values, morals, and standards that most people can't comprehend. We are sinners turned into saints because of our new revelation. Although we may stumble, make mistakes along the way, and sometimes even fall, God is there to help us get back into position.

In this newfound life we become saints. It took me so long to come to grips with that statement alone. Me? Keima, is a saint? It's not so much me that is the saint as it is the God in me that makes me holy. It is the God in us that has rescued us from evil. What He's done for me He will do for you too.

There is power in our prayers. So ask God to reveal to you all that needs to be revealed as you continue this process of living for the Lord. As all worldly things are revealed and you're given insight to heavenly things you will be strengthened by your virtuosity. Be mindful at all times that it's His strength and as long as you keep Him at the forefront you will never be weak.

You will always know that you are more than just your name. You are more than what people think of you. You have a huge impact on the lives of many women and children. God specifically made you to build His Kingdom and to prepare the other Saints for His return. Your job is big even if it is on a small platform. Who am I? Who you are? We are priceless women who were made for a purpose.

Week Five

Ingredients
- Bible
- Notebook
- Pencil/Pen
- Fruits/Vegetables
- Bathing Water
- Drinking Water
- Time
- Commitment
- Faith
- Trust

Concealer is used to hide imperfections of the skin. The enemy tries to conceal from us our true nature of being. On the contrary the sacrifice made by Jesus Christ conceals our sins with His blood and we are made clean. This is our salvation. Living the Word of God and following His Commandments allows us to be delivered from evil thus being delivered from sin. Just as the blood concealed our sin the Holy Spirit will conceal our souls from all evil protecting us and bringing us closer to the Divinity of God.

Day 1 Journaling

Do you feel you are worthy to speak God's Word? What do you believe makes you worthy or unworthy?

Are you ready to follow God when He prompts you to move?

Day 2 Journaling

How do you believe you can mature in faith, love, and holiness?

Day 3 Journaling

Based on maturity in faith, love, and holiness which is derived from the Fear-of-God why is a woman who fears God to be admired?

Day 4 Journaling

What does it mean to be respected as a woman? Are there certain things a woman does or should do to get respect from other women, children, and men? Who do you find worthy to be respected in your own sight? Why? How can respect change your life?

Day 5 Journaling

Romans 8: 26-28 (MSG) "Meanwhile, the moment we get tired in the waiting, God's Spirit is right alongside helping us along. If we don't know how or what to pray, it doesn't matter. He does our praying in and for us, making prayer out of our wordless sighs, our aching groans. He knows us far better than we know ourselves, knows our pregnant condition, and keeps us present before God. That's why we can be so sure that every detail in our lives of love for God is worked into something good."

How can this Scripture help you to know yourself better? How do you find yourself despite the things you experience or go through?

Day 6 Journaling

We are all in a common relationship with Jesus Christ. Now that you know there is no distinction between you and your neighbor how do you feel? Do you feel more or less special?

Day 7 Journaling

How do you plan to participate in this life of God? In what area of your life would you like to receive God's promises? How will you use His blessings on your life to further show others the power in the Kingdom of God? How will these actions distinctively represent who you believe God made you to be?

THE FOUNDATION OF FAITH
(6)

What is Faith?

When I was choosing the chapters to this book and came up with the name The Foundation of Faith I was truly excited to be writing about such a wonderful topic. But when it was time for me to begin I wasn't sure how to explain what it meant to be faithful. I know that sounds absolutely insane but the truth is that although faith is the single most important part of our walk with God, it's really hard to define and capture the essence of what faith is in terms of words.

In order to truly walk with the Lord our faith must be strong. Without it we're just as good as lost. We will start this chapter with the following Scripture, Hebrew 11:1-16.

Hebrews 11:1-16 (MSG) "The fundamental fact of existence is that this trust in God, this faith, is the firm foundation under everything that makes life worth living. It's our handle on what we can't see. The act of faith is what

distinguished our ancestors, set them above the crowd.

By faith, we see the world called into existence by God's word, what we see created by what we don't see.

By an act of faith, Abel brought a better sacrifice to God than Cain. It was what he believed, not what he brought, that made the difference. That's what God noticed and approved as righteous. After all these centuries, that belief continues to catch our notice.

By an act of faith, Enoch skipped death completely. 'They looked all over and couldn't find him because God had taken him.' We know on the basis of reliable testimony that before he was taken 'he pleased God.' It's impossible to please God apart from faith. And why? Because anyone who wants to approach God must believe both that He exists and that He cares enough to respond to those who seek Him.

By faith, Noah built a ship in the middle of dry land. He was warned about something he couldn't see, and acted on what he was told. The result? His family was saved. His act of faith drew a sharp line between the evil of the unbelieving world and the rightness of the believing world. As a result, Noah became intimate with God.

By an act of faith, Abraham said yes to God's call to travel to an unknown place that would become his home. When he left he had no idea where he was going. By an act of faith he lived in the country promised him, lived as a stranger camping in tents. Isaac and Jacob did the same, living under the same promise. Abraham did it by keeping his eye on an unseen city with real, eternal foundations—the City designed and built by God.

By faith, barren Sarah was able to become pregnant, old woman as she was at the time, because she believed the One who made a promise would do what he said. That's how it happened that from one man's dead and shriveled loins there are now people numbering in the millions.

Each one of these people of faith died not yet having in hand what was promised, but still believing. How did they do it? They saw it way off in the distance, waved their greeting, and accepted the fact that they were transients in this world. People who live this way make it plain that they are looking for their true home. If they were homesick for the old country, they could have gone back any time they wanted. But they were after a far better country than that—heaven country. You can see why God is so proud of them, and has a city waiting for them."

You may have heard the saying we move by faith and not by sight. What is meant by that is we are moved by the Holy Spirit and not by what we can see with our physical eyes. In order for us to understand this thing called faith we have to keep our spiritual eye open. We can only do that by our submission to God and willingness to follow in the footsteps of Jesus Christ.

Just because we cannot see God moving in our lives doesn't mean that He is sitting still. He is always working and never idle. I used to have conversations with a very close friend of mine who couldn't understand the faith that I had in our Lord. He would say things like I'm walking in "blind faith". He couldn't understand why or how I could do such a thing considering some of the issues I was faced with in my life.

What he failed to realize, was that my faith in God was not blind faith. My spiritual eye was wide open and I was able to see the bigger picture because I was no longer looking through the two eyes attached to my face. I was looking through the eyes of God. Sometimes it may seem that things unseen are unattainable when in all reality all things are at our fingertips. God is as real as the air we breathe but do not see. He is alive and able to change our lives if we choose to have faith.

There is a story in the Bible about a woman who suffered from a bleeding disorder for twelve years. This woman was in a crowd full of people following Jesus. She had so much faith that God could heal her that she believed that by getting up close enough to Jesus just to touch the hem of his robe she would be healed. That is indeed what happened when she touched his robe. She was healed! She had spent all of her money over the years going from specialist to specialist for help with her condition and to no avail.

When Jesus felt a surge of energy leave Him, He wanted to know who in that crowd had touched Him. His disciples thought He was insane. There were many people in the crowd that had touched Him. He wasn't concerned with just anyone he sought the one who had a special kind of faith. The woman was afraid but she took a chance. Standing her ground she didn't let her fear stop her as she knelt before Him and gave Him her entire story. Jesus told her, "By her faith she was healed."

It was not his physical presence that healed her. He said it was **HER OWN FAITH** that did it. She had long given up hope in being cured by man. She stayed focused on Jesus. No matter how long she had to follow Him she believed He was her only chance at beating this ailment. This woman had exhausted all of her resources. She was at a point in which this was it. If Jesus couldn't heal her she would never be healed. She was determined that walking with Him would turn her entire situation around and it did!

What you believe and what you see with your spiritual eye (in your mind) will manifest itself into your physical life. You have to trust that through God all things are possible. I understand that can be a lot. Believe me I know. Coming from a woman who has dealt with trust and abandonment issues all of my life I can understand how something like trusting a God you can't see would seem hard. It might even seem almost impossible but if you choose to open your heart you will experience the rewards of being faithful.

Closing the Gap

I want you to stop reading right now, and take yourself to a quiet place in your home, office, car, wherever you can and give Him a minute or two of your life. I want you to pray. It doesn't have to be this prayer but pray something similar. Pray something that feels right in your own heart.

Heavenly Father, I come to you right now to first and foremost give thanks to You Father God. I want to thank You for opening my heart to receive your message and for guiding me in the direction of holiness. I pray Father that you touch my heart in a way that it has never been touched before. Daddy God help me to understand Your Will for my life. Allow me to have faith in Your vision and in Your Promises so that every move that I make is all for You. Continue Heavenly Father to move graciously in my life so that I can become the woman that You want me to be. Any place where I am lacking fill that area with what is righteous and holy. If I have problems trusting and believing Your Promises and Your ability to move in my life show me where that issue stems from. I rebuke everything that is hindering me from receiving what You have set in motion for my life. Father I pray that You release me from any mental or emotional issues that are blocking me from increasing in faith. In Jesus Name I pray Amen.

Faith Without Boundaries

When growing in faith it is important that you are honest with yourself about where you are in life and where you'd like to go. Take some time for yourself and really consider what your life has been all about up until this point. Where do you see yourself in the near future? Are you comfortable with who you are in terms of your spirituality right now? Find out if there is anything that would sidetrack you in reaching your full potential? Think about some goals that will enhance your personal relationship with the Lord and how you should go about reaching them.

As you read the Word of God your faith should be increasing every day. In my own walk I've found Scripture to be very valuable to me when trying to understand the importance in believing that God will take care of me. The more I read the Word of God the more I believe in Him and what He can do. As I hear, see, and speak His Word worry has ceased from invading my life. My conscious is clear and I'm able to focus on the only thing that matters in this lifetime, which is God's Love.

It's crucial that we do not put a limit on the things that God is capable of doing. When God be with you there is no one on this earth who can be against you and win. Our faithfulness is a display of loyalty to a lifestyle that leads us to the path of everlasting life. Just a small display of faith can bring us a long way and into God's grace, mercy, and favor.

Faith is a choice to believe that God will work things out for you even when you can't see a solution. If you place boundaries on the things that God can do, you are literally placing yourself inside a small box. Everything is attainable with the help and support of God. As you spiritually mature the desires of your heart begin to change. As that change takes place God notices your faithfulness. Your ambition to reach Him is all the incentive He needs to really start performing miracles in your life.

We have faith because it is the only way to build a strong union with God but in doing that we reap many rewards. When we display strong faith in Our Father we are given a peace beyond all understanding. When adversity shows up attempting to block our path we don't cower away feeling defeated. We continue to move forward smiling and pushing through because we know that we serve a God that will change that situation around in our favor.

With that peace we are given comes happiness. People might ask what you have to be so happy about. They can't see what God has done for you just yet. However, you know because God will show you exactly where He's taking you. There have been many times I have found myself lost and confused trying to figure out what my next step should be. I was worried, afraid, and didn't know what the outcome of my situation would be. When I stepped back and reevaluated my circumstances I realized I had to let God take over. I asked Him to handle my situation and He did just that.

While doing that I can remember one particular time in which He showed me in a dream where I was coming from and where I was going. We lived in the Midwest at the time but even in a state where the winters could be cold and frigate I'd never seen a snow covering the ground in June. We were celebrating Christmas at the beginning of summer. All of my family had driven the hour down to spend the holiday at our house. Everyone was there even my brother Booder who has passed away in June of 2009.

Out of nowhere there was pure chaos amongst our family. Everyone began bickering and arguing. Each one accused the other of doing this or that. Things had quickly gotten out of hand. I tried to calm everyone down but the yelling and hollering just seemed to increase. One of my children was pushed down the stairs but I caught her just in time. Strangely enough I wasn't angry. I was as calm as a cool breeze.

I tried to speak over everyone in a soothing tone but they weren't listening. I kept repeating over and over, "Don't worry, everything is going to be alright. Its' okay, see look even Booder's here. We're fine." No one paid me any attention as they continued assaulting one another verbally.

At some point I couldn't take it anymore I needed to get some peace so I left the house to clear my mind. The roads were covered with snow and ice as I slowly made my way up a small hill near a large church. When I reached the top I was situated directly in front of the entrance of House of God. There were three females standing in the road. I pulled over and was greeted by an elderly woman, a young woman, and a baby.

They were speaking another language that I had never heard before. They were Hispanic but it wasn't Spanish. I didn't see any wings but I knew they were angels. I got out that car standing in the middle of the road with them. I felt an overwhelming peace. The feeling was so strong that I was awakened out of my sleep.

I sat straight up in my bed perplexed by what I'd just felt and seen in the dream. I had no idea what that dream meant. God gave me this dream in March of 2011 when I first moved to Atlanta. January I decided to move to Atlanta from Kansas City and within two months I was gone. Although it wasn't evident to me at the time, my life and my spirit was in shambles. My family was still trying to recover from being rocked to the core by Booder's sudden death. We were all still mourning the loss in our own way almost two years later.

My mind often traveled back to that dream. I couldn't get it out of my head. As I began to grow in faith God started to reveal knowledge and discernment to me. The elements in the dream had already begun to manifest itself into my life. June was a month of pure chaos back in 2009 when tragedy struck and Booder passed away. However, in June of 2011 I was blessed with an ideal job. Now this job wasn't just any job, it was a job that was not too stressful. I have an excellent management team and eventually I was able to work from home, taking the burden away of having to find child care for my three children.

In June of 2012 I gave birth to my fourth child. She brought so much joy to my household. She was truly the greatest blessing I'd had all year. In June of 2013 I decided that it was time to take my life to an entirely new level. I started wrestling with the thought of writing a spiritual self help guide, a memoir of who I was, who I wanted to be, and who I'd become thus far.

In luau of those three very significant events in my life over the past three years at that exact time, I have felt myself progressing rapidly into this new woman of God. I literally went from an infant (the first angel) beginning her walk to a young woman (the second angel) and finally to a virtuous woman of God (the third angel) ready to spread His Word. All because I believed in what He showed me and I trusted in His Word. The Spirit of the Lord showed me as I slept what He was going to do in my life. I trusted and believed in what He had instilled in me during that time.

I had these angels guiding me. I had to be the one who spread the Gospel of our Lord and Savior to my sisters in Christ. As I did this I would be protected. They would give me peace even when in the world there was no peace. All I had to do was seek the Son so I could do work for the Father. I had to have faith in that.

He set everything up accordingly. Had I not had the opportunity to work for my employer I would have never found the time or the confidence to begin my career in writing. God strategically set this up for me so I could reach where I'm at right now. Sitting here in front of this computer testifying to whoever will listen and is able to receive what God is saying through me.

God changed my mind and my heart. He delivered me and showed me love and how to have faith in His Word. He is completing me each day just a little more and before long I can testify that I am made completely whole. We all will be able to testify that truth. We grow into the women God wants us to be. Isn't that what we are all seeking? Growth and maturity.

I truly believe that even in a time when I had little faith God was still working things out on my behalf. He showed me the truth behind everything that I was going through. I was being guided into this life I am living now without me even knowing it. In God's realm a little faith will go a long way. You've got to believe and refuse to take no for an answer.

When we do this all of our prayers will be answered in the right time. We won't need to search outside of ourselves for fulfillment because God will have already placed us in a position to have everything we need at our disposal. We'll remain fearless despite what's going on in the world around us, even when it threatens to uproot us from our comfort zone.

Our faith assures us that we are safe. We are under the protection of a Father who will never leave nor forsake us. We'll handle tough situations according to the Love we know He has for us. Trusting Him in all things current and to come, our faith allows us to continue to smile and push forward. We remain happy and joyful even when trouble is in plain sight. We are unable to be moved because we know the outcome of all of our situations. That outcome is God's blessing, mercy, and favor. Those are the rewards are obtained through faith.

What Will Bring Us Closer To God?

1 Corinthians 13:11-13 (MSG) "When I was an infant at my mother's breast, I gurgled and cooed like any infant. When I grew up, I left those infant ways for good.

We don't yet see things clearly. We're squinting in a fog peering through a mist. But it won't be long before the weather clears and the sun shines bright! We'll see it all then, see it all as clearly as God sees us, knowing Him directly just as He knows us!

But for right now, until that completeness, we have three things to do to lead us toward that consummation: Trust steadily in God, hope unswervingly, love extravagantly. And the best of the three is love."

The best of the three is love. It's amazing just how important love is to our lives. I think about all of the different people I have met over my lifetime and the stories they had shared with me. The single most important thing we had in common was the need to be loved.

We'd done some of the strangest and illogical things to get someone to love us. When all we had to do was just turn to God who was standing right next us, carrying us, rubbing our back as we laid in our beds weeping in the midnight hour and hating our lives.

Be assured however, that to have faith the size of a poppy seed is enough for Him to work with. God will do what every father who loves his daughter unconditionally will do for you and then some. His love can't be measured. And He shows no favoritism when it comes to His children.

I can't stress enough that the work, blessings, and miracles He has performed in my life through my faith, He will do that and more in yours too. He didn't choose me because I was special or better than the next person. He chose me because I made a conscious decision to let Him in. I was convicted by His Word and made certain that my life would be better living it according to His Holy Will.

Our faith in His Holy Word determines the Work that He is able to do in our lives and over our lives. Our faith is what determines our blessings, our faith is the determining factor of the amount of peace we have in our lives. It is our faith in the fact that God can perfect us in this imperfect world that pleases Him and brings joy into our lives.

When building you must to make sure the foundation is strong. If you are getting in shape you have to ensure that your core is strong, which in return improves the health of your back and then your overall body. When you build a home the foundation must be intact so that siding, walls, stairs, windows can all go up without crumbling to the ground. It is the foundation of faith that draws us closer to an abundant and prosperous life. It is that abundance and prosperity that draws other believers and even nonbelievers to us and gives us the opportunity to show God's Power.

Week Six

Ingredients
- Bible
- Notebook
- Pencil/Pen
- Fruits/Vegetables
- Bathing Water
- Drinking Water
- Time
- Commitment
- Faith
- Trust

When making up our faces foundation is one of the most crucial elements for a flawless finish. The great thing about foundation is that it evens out our skin tone and allows the rest of our makeup to stay on longer. The same process occurs when dealing with the foundations of our faith. It is the base of who we are and where we are going. It is the love that sustains us and the basic element for walking in God's Light allowing His Will to Manifest into our world. Faith is the focal point for obtaining His Favor.

Journaling Day 1

Trust is one of the most important aspects in our growing faith in the Lord. Name some ways in which you can gain trust in Our Father. Are there any areas in which you have tried to fix on your own? What information are you lacking in understanding regarding your life, trials, and tribulations? Ask God to show you what you need to learn from any situation that has presented itself to you and how you can move past the past.

Journaling Day 2

Write about a time you've gotten involved in something that you could have trusted God to handle. How do you think Jesus would have handled the situation? Express your thoughts and feelings about that how you handled the situation as opposed to how you believe Jesus would have.

Journaling Day 3

What do you need to do to increase your belief in the Lord? Do you believe everything you see with your own two eyes? I hear people say seeing is believing. Is this true to you? Talk about some things that you don't see but that you know to be true.

Journaling Day 4

We know that our faith in His Word pleases Him. Has your heart been at peace? Have you experienced the Holy Spirit giving you rest and assurance?

Journaling Day 5

Understand that we were sent here to follow Jesus. This means even during times of adversity we must trust and believe that what was written about us is true. Our life story was known before we even made it here to earth. We were destined to live the lives we are living now. We must have faith that ultimately in the end God gets the victory. As long as He's living inside of us we get the victory as well. We are protected even when it doesn't feel like it. Incorporate in your journal your story of protection.

Journaling Day 6

Having faith that life challenges gives us the opportunity to build the Kingdom of God. How will you use your stumbling blocks to draw others closer to Our Lord?

Journaling Day 7

As our faith in Jesus increases we gain a God given wisdom. As you've been moving forward in your faith do you recognize areas in which you have changed? Can you notice anything different or new about yourself and the way you think and analyze this life now? Write in detail every piece of wisdom you have gained from growing in faith.

FAITH WITH WORKS
(7)
James 2:14-20 (ESV)

¹⁴ What good is it, my brothers, if someone says he has faith but does not have works? Can that faith save him? ¹⁵ If a brother or sister is poorly clothed and lacking in daily food, ¹⁶ and one of you says to them, "Go in peace, be warmed and filled," without giving them the things needed for the body, what good is that? ¹⁷ So also faith by itself, if it does not have works, is dead.

¹⁸ But someone will say, "You have faith and I have works." Show me your faith apart from your works, and I will show you my faith by my works. ¹⁹ You believe that God is one; you do well. Even the demons believe—and shudder! ²⁰ Do you want to be shown, you foolish person, that faith apart from works is useless?

When I first started preparing to write this book I was constantly attempting to talk myself out of expressing the grace and mercy God had unleashed in my life. The more I tried to stop myself from doing this project the more I couldn't get it out of my mind. I'd wake up in the middle of the night with a thought or idea, find whatever was available to write on, and begin jotting down the thoughts that were bursting to get out of my head. Before long I had notes everywhere.

I was overwhelmed with what seemed like a mountain of information. I didn't know where to begin. I knew my story would help many women. The problem was I didn't know how to express the love I'd received from the pain I'd experienced. Doubt began to creep in threatening to deter me from my path. I used the only weapon I could, my faith.

I opened my Bible for direction, starting to read faithfully, meditating on the Word of God, praying, and journaling. I stuck with it. My faith wouldn't allow me to waiver from His Word. As I grew in faith, my conviction to believe in what God was urging me to **do** increased as well.

Faith with works was living! As I allowed the Spirit of God to direct me, everything poured out of my soul like a waterfall. The pressure was as strong as a thunderstorm. The Word of God burst onto my computer screen cracking the code of my life. The more I wrote the more I felt the presence of God. The more I did what He was telling me to do the more I was affirmed.

I realized that this was what I was called to do. This book would bring healing and enlightenment to women who were just like me. In life there are no coincidences. When things happen we are to take them in stride recognizing it as an opportunity to give God glory and share our testimony with someone who needs hope. In doing this we obtain His favor for our faithfulness. The things God has started in our lives only become greater when we show His Love in the way He wants us to.

Each and every one of us has a ministry inside of us. We are equipped with everything we need to build the Kingdom of Heaven here on earth. ***Ephesians 4:12 (ESV) "12 to equip the saints for the work of ministry, for building up the body of Christ,"*** It is our works according to our faith that brings us into what God's Purpose is for our lives. Whatever our passions, we are to use them for the greater good of God's Kingdom. We have an obligation to do so.

There are too many hurting people in this world for us as daughters of the Most High God to sit back and allow them to fall into the snares of the devil. We have to stay firm in our faith and pray over ourselves, our children, and even our enemies. Our works is what protects us. Our faith and our works together build us into powerhouses of strength against forces that we don't have the power to fight on our own. Just look at the news. Every day we see something more sinister manifesting into our atmosphere.

God made us all great at something. The spiritual gifts we're given are designed to take our ministries to a very large scale. It's important that we're aware of His Will over our lives. We are given a mixture of tools to use in order to spread the Gospel. You might be wondering what God's Gifts consists of. Let's take some time to discuss each in minor detail.

<u>Wisdom and Knowledge</u>

Ecclesiastes 8:1 (MSG) "There's nothing better than being wise, Knowing how to interpret the

meaning of life. Wisdom puts light in the eyes, and gives gentleness to words and manners."

Many of us experience the same things over and over because we handle "life" the same way each time we're presented with adversity. We mistake wisdom and knowledge with experience. Life's experiences however don't necessarily make us knowledgeable or wise. Unless we've actually learned something from them they're just one of life's trials.

God's gift of wisdom and knowledge is so important to the existence of mankind. When we're strong in the Lord and allow Him to guide us, all of life's mysteries are made clear. The why's we once asked become praises of thanks as our wisdom increases. Wisdom is the key to understanding all that's important in this walk with Christ. In order for us to overcome our obstacles we must be able to understand why we're facing the challenge to begin with. When we recognize the truth behind our trials and tribulations we become equipped with the knowledge necessary to create solutions for our problems. Once we've mastered this for ourselves we can assist others as well.

Each one of us has the gift of wisdom and knowledge. All of us have experienced trials and tribulations that we're able to learn from. We have the ability to make good judgment in handling any situation that could hinder our paths. "Common sense" kicks in and where we once made mistakes we start to tweak our responses for a better outcome.

God gives us knowledge and wisdom so that

we can help one another to overcome "life's" ups and downs. In this book I have consistently spoken about times in my life where I was confused, sad, and angry. In those times I ran to my friends and family to seek advice. Truth is at times we need advice from others for matters we're unable to comprehend. Although I know they meant well, the advice that was given to me a lot of times was worthless. I say worthless because at the time they were basing their wisdom off of their own thoughts and ideas and not using the intelligence that God had instilled inside of them.

So when I followed this advice I'd fall face first because even though on the outside these people "looked" like they had it together, they too were in a state of crisis. They were hurting and holding on to things that were hindering them. Neither of us had taken the time to look up to the Heavens and speak to God on an intimate level. We were bitter about the "hand" we had been dealt in life. The advice that I was given and even the advice that I'd given myself was laced with pain, hatefulness, and most of all unforgiveness.

We were the spiritually blind leading the spiritually blind, trying to find a miracle in the midst of our nonsense. However, when God touches us it's our duty in the form of our testimony to spread His Word. As daughters of the Most High God we have to share this wisdom to others so that they will have hope. We have to show them God's Light in the knowledge that we receive.

I hear the statement," Knowledge is power," often. I agree wholeheartedly, but only God's knowledge has the power to turn our lives around. The world as we know it starts to change when we obtain it. I speak on this with conviction because my life changed because of it. No matter how much knowledge I gained from life, school, etc. it didn't help me until I understood the true meaning of living. We live to love. Love is God. Through love we form a union with our Father, and then unite with our sisters and brothers in His name. That is truly living in selflessness.

Preaching, Teaching, Apostleship, Serving/Ministering and Leadership

In order to take on this role one must be "called". Being called produces a desire inside of you to serve the Lord that is so strong you can't get it off your mind. The commitment that you have towards building the Kingdom becomes undeniable. No matter how hard you try to shake the feeling or how much you try to talk yourself out of doing that "crazy" thing that popped into your head, you just can't. Even if you try to walk away the idea never truly leaves you. A calling is the undying faith and conviction that your purpose is to serve God's people.

Some of us are also given this gift of Leadership and or Apostleship. We can lead by preaching, teaching, and even serving in a ministry. In order for us to master this gift we have to know God and His Truth. For us to know these things it's crucial we search and research His Word through studying, prayer, meditation, and intimate relationship with Him. If God has placed you in this position of authority it is important that as a leader you understand your role. You should accept the fact that although you aren't perfect you shouldn't settle for anything less than perfection in your faithfulness.

    The most important thing about leading is that we approach life just as Jesus did. As leaders there's a certain level of responsibility that God places on us as individuals. We have to keep ourselves and our own personal thoughts and ideas out of the equation and allow God to lead the way. One of the best ways to do this is to constantly give Him the glory in everything we do. Ultimately it's His way that leads us on our journey.

    We must deliver the Truth with a clarity that our students hadn't been able to understand before. We have to meet them exactly where they're at and help them to seek God consistently. This takes a high level of creativity to be able to analyze and break down the Word to reach others in their current state of mind. Even Jesus used parables to break down this lifestyle in a way so that many could understand and receive.

    As women we play a key role in the lives of humanity as a whole. We're designated with carrying "life" inside of our wombs until it's ready to enter this "world". We vow to love, provide, protect, and nurture that life for the rest of their lives. And in some instances we bond with other children, women, and even men who we feel need that nurturing, love, and protection as well. God made us specifically to pull the Love out of others. Jesus says Love is more important than anything else pertaining to this walk. Which is why the sensitive nature of us as women is crucial in ministry?

I can remember I used to say things like, "I'll die for my children." At the time I meant in the physical sense. However, after I became saved I truly understood the significance of the words I'd spoken since I'd become a mother. That death manifested into my life when I died to myself. In dying to ourselves we're given life from the One True Living God. In reality we become more alive than ever. In dying we choose to gain life through Christ. We're able to lead our children to the well of living water. It's us who are designated to build boys and girls into the men and women who will spread the Gospel in the future.

Our job as women is more important than ever. My uncle and I had a debate once. He told me that a woman couldn't tell him anything. God didn't send women onto this earth to preach to a man. At the time I was taken aback. I looked at him like he was crazy. I challenged him to show me where in the Bible it stated that women could not preach the word of God. Although he never gave me the Scripture I took it upon myself to find out if that was true.

1 Timothy 2:11-14 (ESV) *"[11] **Let a woman learn quietly with all submissiveness.** [12] **I do not permit a woman to teach or to exercise authority over a man; rather, she is to remain quiet.** [13] **For Adam was formed first, then Eve;** [14] **and Adam was not deceived, but the woman was deceived and became a transgressor."***

From that point on I had no argument but I was perplexed as to why a man couldn't learn from a woman. I mean after all, Priscilla and Aquila did teach something to Apollos.

Acts 18:24-26 (ESV) *"²⁴ Now a Jew named Apollos, a native of Alexandria, came to Ephesus. <u>He was an eloquent man, competent in the Scriptures.</u> ²⁵ <u>He had been instructed in the way of the Lord. And being fervent in Spirit,</u>¹ <u>he spoke and taught accurately the things concerning Jesus, though he knew only the baptism of John.</u> ²⁶ He began to speak boldly in the synagogue, but when Priscilla and Aquila heard him, <u>they took him aside and explained to him the way of God more accurately."</u>*

At first I thought that this was some kind of contradiction. I couldn't understand how it clearly stated women were to "stay in their place" when it came to preaching and teaching the Word of God, but these women had taught Apollos. Then it dawned on me that our ministries all require teaching. So this reference to women not being able to have "spiritual authority" over men didn't imply women were useless in a man's spiritual growth it's quite the opposite. You see not all males who are grown by physical standards have made it to a state of spiritual maturity.

Scripture says Apollos was, *"Competent in the Scriptures. He had been instructed in the way of the Lord. And being fervent in Spirit, he spoke and taught accurately the things concerning Jesus, though he knew only the baptism of John."* The key to this Scripture is this; *he knew only the baptism of John.* This statement implies that there are indeed levels of spiritual maturity. Apollos had reached one level but it was the calling God put on the hearts of Priscilla and Aquila that gave him what he needed to go to the next level of spirituality.

Also notice that they took him to the side. Their role was not to stand in front of the entire synagogue and "teach" Apollos, but to follow God's order and minister to Him the ways of the Lord in private. Spiritual maturity is not determined by age or gender. Each of us will encounter someone who will help us to get to the next level at some point in our lives. It could be a man, woman, or even a child so we must always remain open to the way of the Lord so that we won't miss what God wants us to receive. As women we should never be afraid to come forth when we're called by God.

As we build our ministries, we will encounter males and females of all ages that we're required to minister to. Yes, as women we will encounter male adults that have not yet matured in Christ. Their receptiveness is based off of our prayers and ability to follow the path God has lain before us. We cannot be afraid to explain His way accurately just as Priscilla and Aquila did in the book of Acts.

God loves His daughters and trusts us just as much as He trusts His sons. Although having spiritual authority over mature men of God is not a role us as women should take on we have so many other roles that help strengthen the Kingdom as a whole. Every day we are practicing Apostleship when we start a new ministry reaching out to those who haven't been able to receive the Gospel.

I know women who have a ministry for health and fitness, even hair salons. You may not recognize a hair salon as a ministry but the Bible says that a woman's hair is her glory. Promoting healthy, strong, and beautiful hair is indeed a ministry. No matter how big or small, how much education you have or don't have, you have a ministry inside of you. Kingdom Work is no small task. Your time and effort never goes unrecognized. You are an important piece to the Kingdom of God.

__Evangelism__

In a world filled with temptation walking the path of righteousness can be tough. At times it can even be discouraging when we're unable to reach others. This is why God gives some of us the gift of evangelism. With this gift the Holy Spirit fills us to our capacity enabling us to spread the Word of God to people who are "harder to reach."

An evangelist discerns spirits and is able to pinpoint specific issues one is facing. Once the issue has been recognized he or she is able to witness to that individual. In doing this there is an undeniable truth that God is working. He has given the evangelist all the tools needed to show His Glory.

An evangelist will have a strong conviction to want everyone to know the good news and have no fear of spreading the Gospel. Doing so brings God's Light to the path of the lost. Each one of us possesses the ability of evangelism to some extent. For some of us it's our calling to reach out to those others consider "lost causes." Truth is no one is truly a lost cause God can work miracles in anyone.

Prophecy

Many times in my life I've had dreams of things that came to pass. Prophecy? Yes but that is only a small part of what being a prophet is. To prophesize is to also speak on behalf of God. There are times when the Holy Spirit moves and compels us to speak for Him to a certain person or group of people to inform them to repent, change their ways and do what is righteous.

Joel 2:28 (NIV) [28] **_"And afterward, I will pour out my Spirit on all people. Your sons and daughters will prophesy, your old men will dream dreams, your young men will see visions."_**

Through our prophesying to one another in the Spirit we're able to change what is called fate or destiny. When we know the truth about what God has in store for us we're able to prepare for anything bad or good that comes our way. In recognizing that God is in control we are given an advantage over the enemy. We're put back on the path we'd started on before He placed us in our mothers' womb. Our purpose in life becomes evident and we can move into all God has for us.

Prophets are needed in order to restore God's order here on earth. The prophetic missions of our prophets and prophetesses are also crucial to building faith. Prophecy not only consists of things to come but it's also our only link to a future of perfect peace.

Faith/Healing/Miracles

We've already talked about building our faith now lets' talk about faith as a ministry. Believing that God will do exactly what He said He'll do despite our ability to see the blessing and favor coming is ministering by faith. It's our faith in God that sets the wheels in motion for the "miracles" we experience in life.

Faith as a ministry is our ability to show others that no matter what's going on in our lives we continue to trust that the Lord will see us through it. Because of that trust God turns our situation into an opportunity to produce a miracle. These miracles become our testimony and our testimony becomes proof that God is real.

With so many sick people in the world today I can only imagine how many miracles of healing God is waiting to perform. This is why knowing who we are, who sent us here, and what we were made to do is so important. This isn't only about physical illness. It's about mental, social, economic, financial, and emotional illnesses as well.

Healing brings us closer to God. When we are physically healed we can then be spiritually healed. In the same instance, when we are spiritually healed we can also be physically healed. They go hand in hand. Without faith we can't move mountains. Without faith we don't have the ability to heal ourselves. If the woman with the bleeding disorder had no faith she couldn't have been healed of her disease. For twelve years she suffered.

I can only imagine how fragile her mental state was because of this. She had to have been weak from losing so much blood. No one could help her with this issue until she increased her faith in Jesus. She was backed against the wall and had no one or nothing else to turn to. So she followed Him. She touched Him. What He told her was it was her faith that ultimately healed her of the ailment she'd been battling. It was her determination that despite the fact that no one could help her in 12 years she didn't give up.

Faith heals; faith makes room for miracles to manifest in our lives. I don't know how many times I've prayed for God to help me provide for my children as a single mother, but because I didn't give up He answered my prayers. I didn't give up because I knew that ALL THINGS were possible if I could just keep the faith despite all the things I'd went through.

God wants and needs to create a miracle in your life. Your faith will heal you not hinder you. It will release you from anything that is keeping you from experiencing "Real Life". We spend so much time looking to fix things when all we have to do is have faith. No struggle we experience in this lifetime belongs to us it belongs to Him.

This is why some of us are designated with an extra strong portion of faith. Faith is contagious. It's something that the person who has it can't see but the person who is looking notices. Faith brings about hope. With hope there is a refusal to give up. That refusal brings about change. The ministry of believing and trusting in God is imperative to the survival of humanity because without faith there is no belief. Without belief there are no believers.

Tongues and Interpretation of Tongues

Acts 2:4 (KJV) "And they were all filled with the Holy Ghost, and began to speak with other tongues, as the Spirit gave them utterance."

Speaking in tongues is an amazing gift from God. When filled with the Holy Spirit of God we are given the ability to talk in other languages. On the day of the Pentecost God sent His Spirit so that the people could be assured that He was with them. They spoke in tongues from all countries with no previous knowledge of those languages before. It was proof that God was real and He was Living.

Even today we are still given the gift. There is one important aspect one should keep in mind however, when speaking in tongues. This is crucial to the ministry of being able to communicate in many languages and that is to ensure that everyone in attendance understands what is being said. There should always be an interpreter available to bless the listeners with what the Holy Spirit has to say to the group. We are all a part of the body of Christ so it's imperative that we work together for the greater good of God. In order to do so we must all be in one accord. Understanding each other and knowing what the work is that needs to be done is the only way for us to become one.

Discernment

This is one of the most wonderful gifts to have. At times we can find ourselves being led by a situation, environment, or even a person and, because we are emotional creatures we act out as opposed to listening to that small voice that tells us to do or not to do something. Sometimes that voice may even warn us about a specific person or act.

Now the Bible is very clear about judging others. However, with the gift of discernment we do have the ability to judge. It doesn't mean we're "passing judgment on a person" but it's something about their spirit that causes our soul to stir, which leads us into what God wants us to do. You're able to tell good from bad, evil from holy, and right from wrong. With that knowledge you can accomplish God's Will for the situation accordingly.

Not only does God give us the ability to discern situations, and people, we're also shown how to discern what is true and false. The Bible distinctively warns us about false prophecy. Therefore it must be a very important topic which I believe we need to touch base on.

1 John 4:1 (MSG) "My dear friends, don't believe everything you hear. Carefully weigh and examine what people tell you. Not everyone who talks about God comes from God. There are a lot of lying preachers loose in the world."

I chose to quote that Scripture from the Message Bible for one distinct reason, when I first started this walk I was bombarded by a lot of information. It was really hard for me to determine the truth from a lie. I battled with myself constantly concerning Jesus, God, and the way I was supposed to live my life.

There was one person who helped me to understand the Word of God in ways I didn't know I was capable of doing. My eyes were opened to the world of "religion." I read a lot of interesting books. In studying these "other" books and religious practices I realized I was becoming more confused than ever.

As God began to work in me the truth about the doctrines I'd studied became clear. I realized those doctrines didn't give me the peace I was seeking. I recognized in searching for the undisputed truth I had lost my way and was in constant turmoil. I did what I thought I needed to do, I sought after this person they called Jesus. When I finally had the chance to meet Him my entire life changed.

Before I met Christ my studying was never done in the Spirit. My focus was off. Most of my studying consisted of discrediting Christianity. I disputed celebrating Christmas in December arguing that Jesus wasn't born on or near that day. I also brought race and ethnicity into the equation by arguing that Jesus was a "black man" and "African Americans" were stripped of their native beliefs when they were brought over to America as slaves. What we should and shouldn't eat, how women should wear their hair, etc. had become a part of my being. I was obsessed with every little minute thing. In the end none of what I was focusing on was relevant to

my peace, joy, and happiness.

Some might ask why these things aren't relevant. First of all God doesn't even work on time as we know it. If that is the case why is the actual time of Jesus' birth important? God never designates a time for anything therefore, it can't be too important. Secondly, it's shown in the New Testament that God is not concerned with "laws". The New Testament focuses solely on direct relationship with God through Salvation. God is not concerned with what we eat or how we cook it. He could care less about how our hair is done. There are more important things to this life. Those things are all spiritual. He focuses on cleaning us from the inside out. The physical is truly irrelevant because if the spiritual is good the physical will be good as well.

The point I'm trying to make in telling this story is as I grew in Christ, I was able to discern what did and didn't matter to God. I saw things for what they were and only spoke goodness and truth as I was able to see through the Holy Spirit. As I work for the Lord I'm able to show God's Love by not focusing on "sin" but focusing on God's Truth, Grace, Love, and Mercy. Love is ultimately the most important thing in life.

Mercy/ Giving/ Exhortation

Colossians 3:12** "12 **Therefore, as God's chosen people, holy and dearly loved, clothe yourselves with compassion, kindness, humility, gentleness and patience."

Every time I think about the spiritual gift of Mercy, I think of doctors, nurses, etc... My mother suffers from spinal stenosis, a condition in which her spine narrows as she ages. She has severe pain at times, numbness, and sometimes she isn't able to control what she wants to do because of the nerve damage caused by the condition.

When she went in to have her first surgery, her recovery was rough. She had a doctor and nurses who had no bed side manner. They were rude and very uncaring. She was depressed during her stay in the hospital and even more upset when she came home. The way her neurologist spoke to her it was as if he could care less about her recovery or healing. She didn't get better within a few years her condition worsened. She decided to find a new doctor and precede with yet another surgery. She was told there would be a 15% chance that she'd be cured.

With this new doctor I saw a newfound hope in her. She went through the surgery at a new hospital with a wonderful staff and her recovery this time was much better. She didn't experience half as much pain as she had with the first surgery and she'd felt better a lot faster. Their compassion had made her feel more at ease.

They listened to her concerns, answered her questions, and remained attentive the entire time. I accredit their mercy to her optimistic outlook the second time around. They had given her hope. The spiritual gift of mercy is used to lead others through compassion and patience.

Acts 20:35 (ESV) "In all things I have shown you that by working hard in this way we must help and remember the words of the Lord Jesus, how he himself said, "It is more blessed to give than receive."

Not too long ago my grandparents came from Kansas to Atlanta to visit. Having not seen them in about two years it felt truly amazing to be in their presence. To my children and me seeing them was as great of a gift as a million dollars. Their presence was so joyful for my family that at one point we all became overwhelmed and began to cry. Spending some quality time with them was a true blessing.

On the last night that they were here my grandmother reached into her purse pulling out two twenty dollar bills handing them to my oldest daughters. My girls tried to decline but my grandmother wouldn't take no for an answer. She told them that it would literally hurt her feelings if they didn't accept her money.

My daughters of course didn't want to hurt their great grandmothers' feelings, so they took the money despite not wanting to. Their reasoning for not wanting to take the money was because they knew our grandparents were on a fixed income and they felt very passionate about not putting them in a financial bind.

On the other hand my grandparents have always been very giving people. Even growing up as a child there was nothing they wouldn't do for their children and grandchildren. They'd always help out with a giving heart even when we made mistakes. Their genuine love for the happiness and wellbeing of others is unlike anything I've ever seen. All the children in the neighborhood call them grandma and grandpa. Their giving is genuine. If they see a child without they take notice and help never expecting anything in return.

We all can agree that when we do something nice or good for someone else we genuinely feel great about ourselves. True giving of time, advice, gifts, food, assistance, etc. brings joy to our hearts. That joy alone is a blessing.

The gift of giving does not only provide blessings to the giver but to the person or person receiving as well. And in a lot of instances as with faith, mercy, prophecy, evangelism, and every other gift we've talked about in this chapter those things lead to exhortation.

When we see God working through others it's encouraging. It lets us know that there is a God and this world isn't always hard and cold. As we follow Christ we're automatically given the gift of exhortation rather we realize it or not. Why should we be encouraged through our walk with God?

1 Thessalonians 5:9-11 (ESV) "9 For God has not destined us for wrath, but to obtain salvation through our Lord Jesus Christ, 10 who died for us so that whether we are awake or asleep we might live with him. 11 Therefore encourage one another and build one another up, just as you are doing."

As Gods people we need our self-esteem back. Like a boxer in a boxing ring we need not to be afraid of looking our opponent in the eye. We have to be willing to strike hard enough to obtain the knockout. This is how we have to be with our new life in Christ. We need our trainer in our corner encouraging us letting us know that it doesn't matter what it looks like to anyone else in the world we're winning.

    If we have a vision God will bring it to fruition. All we have to do is believe that He is real and His power is real. It's simple; we just do what it is we were called to do. Using our spiritual gifts and waiting for God to direct us gives us a sense of accomplishment. Through doing good deeds resulting in the completion of the Will of God in our lives we are exalted to the next level of spiritual maturity. That's incomparable to anything we can ever receive. We should all be grateful for that blessing.

Week Seven

Ingredients
- Bible
- Notebook
- Pencil/Pen
- Fruits/Vegetables
- Bathing Water
- Drinking Water
- Time
- Commitment
- Faith
- Trust

As the Nike Slogan says, "Just Do It." Anytime we are blessed with an idea, a dream, an ambition, we shouldn't just sit on it and never move we have to get to work. If we want to lose weight what do we do? We work out! If we want to become a medical doctor, what do we do? We go to college and then to medical school, preparing for a career in medicine! When we speak the Word of God in hopes that others will join into the body of Christ, what do we do? We use our spiritual gifts to create ministries, encourage God's people, give them hope, show them mercy, and prophesy over their lives, we show random acts of kindness and generosity, we build a fire amongst the saints. We work to build the faith of our own people so that the Light will shine brightly over the world bringing everything back to its natural order.

Sunday-Saturday

Colossians 3:23 (NIV) "Whatever you do, work at it with all your heart, as working for the Lord, not for human masters."

This entire week it is important to journal about the work that you do. Think about your job and try to find some ways in which you can show God's Love through your work. Also consider all of the spiritual gifts God gives to us. Which gift do you feel most appropriately matches you as an individual person.

Are there any ministries that you are interested in becoming involved in or even venturing out on your own with? This week I want you to think of the ways you can incorporate your faith into action. Plan and begin to bring your thoughts, ideas, etc. into fruition by, "Just Doing It!"

Remember allowing God to work through you does not have to be anything extravagant. It can be something as simple as a, "God bless you today," towards a perfect stranger, a prayer with someone who is feeling down, donating things you don't use anymore to a charity, giving a homeless person something to eat. Any act of kindness and compassion is pleasing to God.

Everyday take the time out to consciously do one "good" thing for someone else and write about it in your journal.

THE COLOR OF VIRTUE
(8)

Humility: the quality or state of not thinking you are better than other people: the quality or state of being humble.–Merriam Webster Dictionary

This chapter has been one of my favorites to write because it's allowed me to be a little creative. If there's anything that I love the most about learning the Word of God, it's understanding Scripture from multiple standpoints. What better way to explain why humility is so virtuous than through color scheme?

I've described several colors in a way that displays the things we go through as women and how they contribute to our virtuosity. They represent the different aspects of our spiritual being. The color of our life builds us into beautiful women of virtue who hear, speak, and see things in the Spirit. We represent ourselves in the likeness of God even when no one else is watching. We don't do this with pride on our tongues or in our hearts. We don't boast about where God has taken us instead we encourage each other. We come to each other as servants of the Lord to help one another reach our highest potential as women of God. We're humble knowing that we aren't worthy of the grace and mercy that He has given us yet we received the gift anyway. For our continued faithfulness we inherit His Kingdom.

Through our humility we are able to receive the knowledge He has for us and continue to have blessings and favor rained down upon us. We have to let go of our pride to come into what was made for us. We have to know and understand that it is our humbleness that prepares us to live the life God intended for us to live. To obtain that humbleness there are several things we must understand. These colors will give you a clear picture in how to humble yourself into blessings and favor.

BLACK: Understanding times of darkness

There's a story in the Bible about two blind men faithfully seeking Jesus. Physically they can't see Him, yet they trail behind Him for quite some time anticipating being healed by Him. They never stray away. Although their blindness made the path very dark they believed in the end the Son of God would bless them with sight. Their faith was strong although they couldn't see the light at the end of their journey.

They didn't have to see Him to know that God was able to give them what they needed. They listened to the Word which led them to a place where Jesus could heal them. The darkness that they lived in was ultimately what brought them to the light.

***Genesis 1:1-2 (MSG)** "1-2 First this: God created the Heavens and Earth—all you see, all you don't see. Earth was a soup of nothingness, a bottomless emptiness, an inky blackness.*

God's Spirit brooded like a bird above the watery abyss."

Darkness can come in the form of our own thoughts, environment, or circumstances. A lot of times in our darkness we are mourning over something we believe is gone because we can no longer see it. We may have been in the darkness for so long that we adapt to being hidden from the light. We stay there for fear of seeing what truly lies ahead of us based off of our past experiences.

What once felt wrong begins to feel right. We get complacent with our situation and become bitter and hateful bringing us on the brink of death. We feel alone and empty. We've changed into our all black attire and darkness represents our lost hope.

On several occasions the Bible speaks about "darkness". In the beginning before there was Adam and Eve, day or night, water and land, there was darkness. In that darkness hovered God. Through that darkness God brought forth, the heavens and the earth, water and land, light, plants, animals, even human beings. With God was strength, love, protection, shelter, hope, and an abundance of many other things including **change**.

Had the blind men been able to see would they have followed Jesus into the house allowing Him to work a miracle within their lives? Had we never experienced any adversity in our own lives would we have come to know God for ourselves? I personally believe that had I not dug myself into a deep hole every time I tried to fix something in my life that I messed up, I would've never had an intimate relationship with the Lord. It's comforting to know that even in our darkest hour God is hovering over us just as He hovered in the very beginning. He's patiently waiting to make something out of nothing.

Let's take off our funeral apparel and liven our wardrobe. Let's grow from plain seeds buried in soil into lively plants that produce oxygen for living. Experience the endless possibilities of life. Accept the darkness and wait for it to bring forth God's Light. As He hovers near in your darkest hour recognize He's only preparing you for the next phase in your life.

BLUE: Faith in God's Lifeline

Ephesians 2:8-9 (ESV) "For by grace you have been saved through faith. And this is not your own doing; it is the gift of God, not a result of works, so that no one may boast."

Yes, God does a whole lot of saving and it's not because you are you it's because He wants to give His children gifts. God is a loving parent who takes pleasure in seeing His children in a peaceful, loving, and joyful place. We please God through our faith and trust in His Word. Through following His Son, Jesus, we increase in both of these things.

The thing about faith is it brings on an entirely new meaning to our lives. Faith isn't something that we can literally go out to get we have to train ourselves into learning Scripture and obtaining what we call "God Intelligence."

With this intelligence we obtain from God there comes a natural order. Things that we used to be okay with doing and saying doesn't feel right anymore. It's not because those things were something that we were naturally used to doing it's because those are things that we were habitually used to doing. When God informs us however, we become knowledgeable of their potential to lead us into sin.

I liked to think of myself as a pretty good person even before I was saved. However, when I began to mature in Christ I began to see things in a different light. It wasn't enough to be a "good person". I saw that my faith in the Lord had to increase tremendously. When I dove head first into the Word I saw how having faith created a security within myself I never knew was possible.

As a woman who was once quick to become angry and have mundane disputes, I found myself calm when faced with adversity. It was so funny because people who thought they knew me would look at me and say, "What's wrong with you?" My response would always be nothing. They thought that I was being sarcastic when in reality the natural order of my being had been restored inside of me. There wasn't anything that was wrong with me. Negativity didn't consume me anymore because I "knew better".

I didn't understand what I was going through but because of my faith I allowed it to "be". What I was feeling wasn't forced I knew my life was finally calm. For the very first time ever I experienced a genuine peace engulfing me. I welcomed it stopping the search for it and allowing it to just envelop me through my faith. Through that peace of mind, developed "True Love".

Isaiah 26:3 (NIV) "You will keep in perfect peace those whose minds are steadfast, because they trust in you."

RED: Understanding His True Love

Being in Love with Love, mm mm mm. I smile as I write these words. When we find this Love called God the feeling in indescribable. When I was introduced to Jesus, I felt the Holy Spirit filling my body from the crown of my head to the soles of my feet. It wasn't the puppy love from the seventh grade. This was real. I had a tingling deep down inside the very fiber of my being. Nothing or no one had ever made me feel so great! I was all in.

Life as I knew it was over and I refused to go back to my old ways. I'd knew of God before, but to experience Him was intense and enlightening. The assurance the Holy Spirit gave me led me to be at peace with things I'd thought I needed to understand for years.

Because of this Love my spirit is moved to share His Word with anyone who will listen. It was His Word that fed me and guided me from darkness, into a never ending sky of opportunity, through His Love. That Love gives us passion to do His Will. It grows inside of us each and every day we wake up and give Him the glory. We become determined to truly live life. There's an urgency to speak Scripture over the lives of our brothers and sisters that we develop through this Love. Love is not a feeling that comes and goes it is a being. In that being we decide to display kindness, patience, humility, trust, faith, selflessness, and to meet the needs of others without reciprocation. Love connects the spirit to the soul, and the soul to the flesh, allowing the flesh to overcome sin.

1 Corinthians 13:4-8 (NIV) "4 Love is patient, love is kind. It does not envy, it does not boast, it is not proud. 5 It does not dishonor others, it is not self-seeking, it is not easily angered, it keeps no record of wrongs. 6 Love does not delight in evil but rejoices with the truth. 7 It always protects, always trusts, always hopes, always perseveres. 8 Love never fails. But where there are prophecies, they will cease; where there are tongues, they will be stilled; where there is knowledge, it will pass away."

Believe in this kind of love my sisters. Practice this love and be this love. It is not only of great benefit to you but to each and every person around you as well.

GREEN: Finding Balance in an Unbalanced World

Matthew 11"28-30 (ESV) "Come to me, all who labor and are heavy laden, and I will give you rest. Take my yoke upon you, and learn from me, for I am gentle and lowly in heart, and you will find rest for your souls. For my yoke is easy, and my burden is light."

Where I was once tired and drained not from anything in particular but life, He gave me supernatural strength. He made my days seem longer because I was getting everything I needed and still having a good nights' rest. I'd wake up refreshed, fully charged, and ready to move into an entirely different zone.

Being a single mother of four is not an easy task. I work fulltime for an employer, write at least 25 hours per week, sell hand knitted blankets, in addition to cooking, cleaning, and anything else that needs to get done, used to leave me spent. But, God! He's kept me sane and happy through all these days of nonstop work. Being able to focus on His Love has given me the opportunity to see firsthand how light His Burden truly is.

With this newfound love comes balance. Who doesn't need balance and unity in their lives in this day and age? The hustle and bustle of day to day life doesn't exempt anyone. I am amazed at how fast everything is moving in our lives at the exact same time.

There are cars speeding down highways, people talking and texting on cellphones, rushing into offices, schools, grocery stores, everyone seems to be doing something all the time. While this doesn't necessarily have to be a bad thing, I recognize the importance of balance in our lives.

In working on this book for the past year I am grateful that the Lord has created a real balance in my life. Had it not been for His opened arms I know that at some point discouragement would've settled in and this project would never have been finished. But God has a way of fixing problems when we're focused solely on His Work.

Instead of us being all over the place with our ideas, goals, and aspirations we should create a balance for our path. That balance is God. If God is in the forefront of everything we do, our lives become aligned and we're able to avoid many of life's detours.

YELLOW: Allowing the Son to Shine His Light

Now that our lives are fresh and new we have a sense of comfort and confidence when faced with adversity. When something goes wrong we can remain optimistic in our views. That optimism shines brighter than the darkness that intends to corner us. We know that we are walking a path of righteousness and the rewards of this walk are endless. Our assurance comes by way of Jesus Christ dying on the cross for our sins.

Our issues are the enemies plot against us to remove us from God's grace. He can't be pleased if we don't have faith in Him. When we forget that He is in control of all things and begin to worry and try to take things in our own hands our faith is reduced. Without that faith and hope a miracle cannot happen.

No matter how big or small every time God moves in our lives it is a miracle and we should be thankful not just for the "big things" but the "small" as well. It is a miracle that our sin has not crippled us to the point we cannot function on a day to day basis. The wages of sin is death so if that is so we are dying slowly and silently every time we transgress against God's Holiness and do not repent and walk away from it.

Because of the Son, we don't have to die. We can overcome sin and walk in righteousness. We are born again and cleared of every transgression we have committed. We can live again and this time to our full potential. Jesus offers us the opportunity to live our lives in the spiritual. When we walk in the Holy Spirit all things great are attainable. As the sunrays shine down upon us physically the Son of God shines through us spiritually as we grow and develop. Through this growth we are made healthy and strong.

ORANGE: Letting Go of What's Old and Accepting all that is New

Our bodies are being replenished by the Living Water provided by following, Jesus Christ. Like a withered plant being nursed back to health we go from dying to thriving with life. We are colorful and able to produce oxygen (life) to others. Not through our own strength but through the strength of the Holy Spirit that is now dwelling within us.

In this new birth we have experienced there is a youthfulness in us that is brought to the forefront. We are excited about who we are and what we can accomplish for Our Father. Sometimes at night we find it difficult to sleep because our minds are going a thousand miles per hour only this time we are not concerned with bills or the troubles of tomorrow but of the gift of life we can share tomorrow.

We become more attractive to the people around us. This is not a "physical attraction" it is spiritual. Our true beauty starts to shine from the inside out. People begin to take notice of you who normally didn't. They can't explain what it is about you but they are drawn to you.

Know that it isn't necessarily you that they're drawn to. It's the Holy Spirit that's living inside of you that beckons them back to their original nature. With attracting those who are perceptible to the message of Our Lord, you'll also be approached by those who are not. In living this new life in the Spirit we must stay covered by the Armor of God at all times. We'll talk about this armor a little later in the book.

PINK: Forgiveness through Compassion and Kindness

With this new you, you will find a new sense of humanity has developed deep inside of your soul. I'm not sure when it happened but at some point in my life I'd become hardened from life's experiences. The more adversity I was faced with the more my heart hardened towards others.

These others didn't necessarily have to have done anything wrong towards me, I just stopped liking people. I was under the impression that people would always hurt you, especially the ones that you trusted to be a pivotal part of your life. Their ultimate goal was to make you believe they were your friend and had your best interest at heart but it was a lie. Nobody was my friend. I was my only friend and didn't need anyone else.

I pushed people away. I would only allow them to get so close to me before I did something to them to get them out of my life. When they had problems and were looking for a true friend to confide in I would tell them to suck it up, stop crying, and move on. I'd taunt them about the way they felt. I had no compassion for what they were going through.

To be honest I wasn't a good friend. I cared about them to a certain extent but when it was all said and done I couldn't have truly cared for them if I refused to trust them. Could I? No, I couldn't. The base of all relationships is trust.

Following Jesus however provided me not only with the ability to trust again but with a new sense of compassion for others. I was sitting down watching the Passions of Christ one day. I'd seen this movie once before many years ago. I couldn't watch all of it though because it angered me so bad. I literally felt hate towards those who had beat and tortured Jesus.

You know you hear the story and it's like, "Oh yeah, Jesus died for our sins. He was crucified. Yeah yeah yeah." But when it was brought to the screen for me to see, I developed a new sense of what that meant. As I sat down watching what Jesus endured for me the tears flowed like a river. However, those tears weren't just flowing for the physical torture that

God sent His Son to endure for us. They flowed for people in general. Not just believers but the Pharisees and nonbelievers too.

I understood why Jesus prayed for them. I recognized his compassion, kindness, and sympathy towards others. Even those who were considered his enemies he blessed them. Everything began to make sense. I now felt this same compassion towards people who I believed have become my enemies. I prayed hard for them in the Spirit so that I could release them from my heart of unforgiveness.

My children always ask me why I cry? I tell them because I feel the pain of people and I can't help but to care about their wellbeing. I see the strippers, the drug dealers, the murderers and I feel their hurt. I sense their emptiness. Those that no one wants to be bothered with, I pray for them because if God had high hopes for me, I know He has high hopes for them as well. The racists that I thought were the scum of the earth because they raped and enslaved my ancestors I pray for them and their souls.

My father who left me before I ever had a chance to prove that I was worthy to be loved by him I pray for him as well. I sympathize with the reasoning that he too may have been fatherless. He too may have been empty; he too may be struggling with issues right now that don't allow him to be a part of my life. I pray for him because God said, that "we reap what we sow."

If that's true I need to pray for my father. I need to have compassion and sympathy towards my father here on earth. If he should ever need me I need to be able to donate a kidney if it means sparing his life. I can't do that if I have no compassion. So this gift, this peace that comes with knowing Him is the best thing that we can ever be given in life. To be able to let go and not hold on to what has the potential to destroy our present and future as it seemingly destroyed our past.

This ability to hope, pray, and help build better relationships among people is amazing. It takes so much strain off of the everyday living. It may have been the prayers of others for me who kept me from falling deeper than I already had.

PURPLE: Knowing You Have a Royal Bloodline

Purple is the color of royalty. Do you understand that you're related to the King of Kings? Do you understand that God created you as a unique, one of a kind individual? He knows everything about you and He watches over you every second of every day? This confirms that you were meant to live a royal life. Sure you've been through the trenches but if dreams weren't an extension of reality we wouldn't have them.

Be convicted and affirmed right now in this moment that you were meant to live a luxurious life. When I say luxurious life I mean exactly that. I want you to declare and decree over yourself right now.

I declare and decree right now over my life prosperity. I declare that not only will I be prosperous in my finances but I'll always have prosperity spiritually, mentally, physically, and emotionally as well. I'll grow in the ways of the Lord so that I can do amazing things that will glorify Our Father in Heaven. I will do His Will here on earth and build up every man, woman, and child so as to bring peace upon this world. I'll do my part in bringing God's children into unity with one another. I will start in my own household, rearing up my children to be young women and men of God. Those children will then go to school and prosper academically and spiritually passing the Holy Spirit of God to their classmates, teachers, and administrative leaders. In return they will take this Holy Spirit home to their own families, to their co-workers, to our government bringing prayer back into our schools, places of business, and into the streets where people find it hard to see God. Father God I decree that any economic hardship that I am going through is over. God has supernaturally put me in a position in which I don't have to worry about where my next meal is coming from. I don't have to be concerned with my children needing new clothes or shoes for school. I declare that God will place someone in my life to fellowship with whom I can be encouraged and in return encourage them. Father God I declare and decree that my bills are paid! I declare and decree that my health is good. Any illness or disease that is forming in my body I rebuke it in the name of Jesus and am healed. If it is not Your Will to heal me in this moment or the next Father God, I am in agreement with You and accept Your Holy Will. I declare that through the trials and tribulations that I go through I will recognize the testimony you are building for me through the test. I will use that testimony to help build the kingdom of God so that the next woman or man or child will not be afraid to face what I'm facing because they know that You're there. Father God I pray for the creativity needed to reach my brothers and sisters in a day and age where we are living in chaos nonstop. In a day and age of confusion about truth I pray that You bless me with knowledge to deliver the Word and to do the Will of Our Lord. I pray not only for the world to change Lord God but for our minds to change while living in this world. I know that You are able to start this domino effect. In Jesus Name I pray. Amen.

As children of the Most High God we can speak these things with authority and have them come to pass. God wants the most for His children. He will not spare any expense when we are obedient and know who we are and where we come from. All we have to do is know that we carry the blood of royalty.

WHITE: The Perfection of Living in Him

We've finally made it to white. White although it doesn't look like it has any color is actually made up of a whole spectrum of colors. So white will represent our wholeness in the Lord. We have come to completion in knowing what it is to be a woman of God. We understand what it takes and we set out to perfect it.

How are we perfect? We're humans we make mistakes right? You are correct in knowing that none of us can be perfect on our own. You are also correct in acknowledging we all make mistakes. It's not in the mistake that brings about the issue. It's our mental capability of accepting that we've made the mistake of committing sin and declaring we will move forward and out of it. We won't beat ourselves up about it allowing it to become a part of who we are.

We come to understand that once we've been saved we become clean and innocent of any guilt. We're balanced in all aspects of our life as every color in the spectrum of colors now illuminates from us. God can truly begin perfecting us in His likeness.

Here's the catch, this isn't perfection of yourself but it's you made perfect through your perfect Father. **Matthew 5:48 (ESV) "You therefore must be perfect, as your heavenly Father is perfect."**

The focus at hand is overcoming your flesh. As our flesh is sinful by nature we must realize although this fight isn't easy with God it is a battle that can be won.

1 Corinthians 10:13 (ESV) "No temptation has overtaken you that is not common to man. God is faithful, and He will not let you be tempted beyond your ability, but with the temptation He will also provide the way of escape, that you may be able to endure it."

There's no need to become discouraged regarding your imperfections as an individual woman. Continue to allow God to remove and replace anything that causes you to lack in His ways. God has the power to move you away from temptation. He is faithful and refuses to give up on you and knows how much you can endure. Remember if He brought you to it He will bring you through it.

Because, we are now perfect and pure through

salvation, prayer, and His Word which is Scripture. These things direct us so that we're on the right path. When we pray we have to understand what it is we need to pray for. No worries ladies. We got this! Keep pushing forward no matter how many times you fall.

Regarding our prayers, God wants us to talk to Him about everything. Our prayers should be selfless. When we pray for one thing and God does something else we shouldn't become angry. We need to trust that He knows exactly what He's doing. Our ultimate goal is to glorify His Name and build up His Kingdom.

Why ask why when God is giving you what you need? It doesn't matter how He gives it you as long as the happiness you asked for is obtained. If you pray for God to give you a happy and healthy relationship and he removes the man YOU thought was your soul mate trust that God has something better for you. Don't continue to hold on to something God said you don't need anymore. It will only cause you unnecessary grief. You are a new woman and with becoming new you have new beginnings.

Always be specific when praying. I find it helpful for me to ask God to give me revelation over the things in my life that need to be perfected. Taking it even a step further I ask God to show me what I need to do to increase where I'm lacking. Last but not least I praise and glorify Him in all that is going on in my life.

When we are becoming perfected in the Lord we have to look for Him in everything. I had someone call me a "Jesus Freak" not too long ago and I think that he was trying to be rude but I was not taken aback. It was God's way of showing me that I was on the right path. I have been able to get to a point where I can see Him in all things and that is when the true blessings begin to rain down upon you.

We see a lot of chaos and madness everyday on our televisions, hear about it on the radio, at times it may present itself directly in front of us, but God is in it all. Please don't be confused, God doesn't want us to live in this kind of world but there is a battle right now for our souls. Jesus was sent here to show us the loving, caring, and nurturing side of our Father. The direct relationship with Him comes through submission, supplication, and fear of Him. When I say fear I don't mean trembling fear of His wrath. I mean fear as in we respect Him so much that we fear disappointing Him because it brings us so much joy to please Him.

None of what is happening in this world can happen without God's permission. We have the free will to do whatever it is that we want to do and He knows that. Therefore as opposed to condemning us He makes sure that in our mission there is a way out. Once we've found His hand we can gravitate towards Him and into His Will for our lives. He is our protection from a society that is out of control.

We have license to carry and stand our ground laws allowing people to obtain and use weapons of mass destruction to "protect them". These weapons are needed why? To protect? They are used to protect because people are living in fear. The Bible says hundreds of times, DO NOT FEAR. We choose to be afraid when we choose to not know God. Fear is not of God.

Recognize the Holy Spirit is living in us, it's a part of us, and if it's a part of us, then it is us and we are it. Ladies it is time for us to act accordingly. We are one, the Father is us because of the Holy Spirit, and we are the Father because His Spirit lives inside of us, we make up the body of Christ here on earth.

All action starts as a thought in our mind. **1 Corinthians 2:11 (ESV) *"For who knows a person's thoughts except the spirit of that person, which is in him? So also no one comprehends the thoughts of God except the Spirit of God."*** Stay filled with His Spirit and all things will be known to you and there will be no surprises in this life that you cannot handle sister. Understand that you aren't just your name; you are a soldier in an army that works to aide in saving souls.

Week Eight

Ingredients
- Bible
- Notebook
- Pencil/Pen
- Fruits/Vegetables
- Bathing Water
- Drinking Water
- Time
- Commitment
- Faith
- Trust

We tend to blush when we are embarrassed, shameful, and even when we're given compliments. Our faces flush and become hot as we try to hide our emotions. Did you know that God loves this? He marvels in the fact that we are not boastful or egotistical. He is even more pleased when we come to Him for help with even the smallest things. Then He knows that we understand we can do nothing on our own.

Day 1 Journaling

Write in your journal about a time. Were you brought out of a dark period? Can you recognize what God was trying to show you at that time in your life? Can you find a Scripture that coincides with the lesson you were taught at that time? Speak this Scripture over yourself.

Day 2 Journaling

John 3:16 (ESV) "For God so loved the world, the He gave His only Son, that whoever believes in Him should not perish but have eternal life."

God sent His Son to die for our sins. I have four children of my own and can truly say I'd rather die for my children than to sacrifice them for the lives of others. It took a lot a lot of Love for God to do such a thing. Think about the first time you thought you were in love. Can you tell the difference between that love and God's Love? What separates God's Love from the love you feel coming from or giving to anyone else? Speak to someone about God's Love.

Day 3 Journaling

Balance in our lives is extremely important. Consider some areas in which you feel take away from your time with God, your family, or from something you enjoy doing. Now take a moment to ponder on some ways you can get this done faster or more efficiently in order to free up more of your time. Pray for wisdom in this area of your life. Write how you would spend that extra 15, 30, or even 60 minutes of your time. Does this coincide with God's Will for your life?

Day 4 Journaling

Proverbs 4:23 (ESV) "Keep your heart with all vigilance, for from it flow the springs of life."

Think of something that brings you down and causes you to worry. Write it down. Now think of ways you can change your thinking towards that situation. After you've done that consider some things you can do right now, today to bring about change in that situation. It doesn't have to be something that will completely turn things around today but what will change this situation over the long run? Has there been anything that you have been doing to feed this situation? Where can you find God in it?

<u>Day 5 Journaling</u>

Proverbs 17:22 (ESV) "A joyful heart is good medicine, but a crushed spirit dries up the bones."

Take some time to speak to your heart mentally, spiritually, emotionally, and physically. Today write about loving yourself and why you are worthy to be loved. I also want you thank God for making you in His Image. Take a few minutes out of your day to exercise your heart in His Love.

<u>Day 6 Journaling</u>

Colossians 3:12 (ESV) "Put on then, as God's chosen ones, holy and beloved, compassionate hearts, kindness, humility, meekness, and patience,"

Find someone anyone and share your kindness with them. Speak life over them today. Allow the Spirit of God to move through you and direct you to someone who needs an uplifting word of encouragement today. Write about the experience.

Day 7 Journaling

As you've started to make some significant changes in your life over the past several weeks have you noticed anything different about the direction you are now going? Have you been able to distinctly see where God has blessed you? Are you able to confidently speak His promises over you and your family and watch them be brought into fruition? Can you see what God is doing in your life right now?

INSIGHT TO SEE
(9)

Blurry Lenses

Matthew 6:22 (ESV) "The eye is the lamp of the body. So, if your eye is healthy, your whole body will be full of light."

As women we tend to look at things from an emotional standpoint. Sometimes we see things not for what they are but for what we feel they are. We see life as a competition and become concerned with what the next woman has or doesn't have. This concern is usually expressed in the form of gossip and is encouraged by other women who envy another as well. They become so engrossed in what that woman has that they themselves become stagnated. They're so busy worrying about someone else's life that they miss their own opportunity to fly first class into God's Favor. The plane has taken off heading towards their destination without them.

I'm sure at some point in time we have all been guilty of this. Truth is this plane was supposed to transport us into broader horizons. Our flight was intended to bring us to a destination of growth and understanding of life's experiences. It took off without us. We were looking at the woman next to us for too long.

As we were running trying to keep up with her we tripped over a log in the road falling flat to our faces. What happened when we fell? We became angry because she got too far ahead of us making us feel as if we couldn't catch up. In that moment we began to speculate. We started to see things through jealous and envious eyes. Blurred visions of hate kept us in a state of confusion.

The fact is she was running the race fair and square looking ahead at what God had waiting for her. Even when she was slightly behind she stopped to help another person get back into the race. We lost not because of anything she did but because we were worried about the wrong thing. As we were getting over the sting of falling she passed us up along with the one she had helped two miles back.

We became desperate to get back into the race of what we presumed to be life. We looked at everyone else's blessings angry that they weren't ours. We didn't see what they went through to get to where they were. We just saw what we wanted and were willing to do whatever it took to get it. The smoke screen was up.

Our own desperation put us into survival mode. When in survival mode we believe we only have one of two choices flight or fight. But what if there were no true danger? What if there was no such thing as losing at life? What if there was no situation that we didn't have the power to overcome? The power of succeeding in life lies in our vision to mentally and spiritually see change manifesting into it.

Competition No More

When we are given insight to the true meaning of living, we'll find that the "race" we were once running is irrelevant. We have no need to compete against one another because in the eyes of God we are all part of one body. It's important that we work together to build the Kingdom of Heaven. Without Christ the head we cannot see where we're going. Without our feet it's harder to walk and without our fingers, hands, and arms it's almost impossible to lift up our fellow sisters and brothers in Christ.

Competition completely goes against the Will of God in our lives. God distinctly tells us not to compete to be better than someone else but to lend a helping hand to others who have fallen behind. This leads back to humility. We don't boast and brag about the things that we've accomplished, instead we look back to see if anyone needs help. Now that we've been exalted into a position to assist others it's our duty to look after one another.

God made you in His Image; therefore, you have the ability to see life as He sees it. It's not the physical eye that gives us this sight it's the Holy Spirit. It's our faith that opens our spiritual eye and connects our souls to the One True Living God.

When we follow Him our path is illuminated with light and we're able to see things more clearly. God will give us the insight that is needed to keep us from walking into temptation and on the path of righteousness. He makes it easy for us to recognize what has always been right in front of us and gives us the ability to bypass anything that will hinder our travel through life. There's no competition, only purpose and each one of us has one.

Jeremiah 29:11 (ESV) "For I know the plans I have for you, declares the Lord, plans for welfare and not for evil, to give you a future and hope." God already knows where He wants you to be and when He wants you to be there. It doesn't matter what it looks like God is able to make things work out in our favor. There was a lesson you learned during your trial rather you realize it or not. Having experienced being molested, raped, in an abusive marriage, and even abusing myself I learned that there was more to me than my experiences.

When I looked at the events of my past from a negative standpoint my life became one big cesspool of pain. However, when I started to recognize God's strength even in my lowest points I was able to come out of my depression. That self-hate and turmoil I'd been experiencing turned into perfect peace. In Him I developed authority over things I couldn't control.

Those men who used me for their own sexual gratification no longer held my heart and mind in captivity. I didn't question those relationships anymore. God helped me see "True Love". He allowed me to envision Love as Him bringing me into the understanding of right and wrong. With that understanding the hope for a better future was established.

Revelation the Beginning of the End

My past was not a part of me, it was a part of life that would move me into the position that God had prepared for me. None of us were created to take up space. We all come with a purpose regardless of our pasts. **Romans 8:28 (ESV) "And we know that for those who love God <u>all things</u> work together for good, for those who are called according to His purpose."**

It can be hard to accept the pain of your past but there's a purpose for it. You didn't live through that pain and loss so you could hold on to it for life and then die with it. You lived through it because you needed it to help another person get through theirs. In order for you to do His Will in their life you have to understand and see that you were made for that experience. No one could've made it through like you did.

Envision yourself in the Spirit and through the eyes of God. His sight is the only true sight. His sight will be your insight to the life you were born to live. Allow what you see in the Spirit to manifest into reality. Never refuse to move forward because of your past. Seeing ourselves in darkness is only a plot from the enemy to keep us in bondage.

While here on earth we're going to experience battles. We may have to fight until we feel as if we are on the brink of death. Once we recognize Who our battles belong to and what they are used for we can move into the beginning of our new lives and lay our old ones to rest.

Our True Identity

1 Samuel 16:7 (NIV) "But the Lord said to Samuel, 'Do not consider his appearance or his height, for I have rejected him. The LORD does not look at the things people look at. People look at the outward appearance, but the Lord looks at the heart."

We are born with the gift of spiritual insight however; the ways of the world taint this insight on a daily basis. What we see going on pushes us further from the spiritual sight of God. In order for us to stay alert and aware of what is truly going on we have to remain in constant contact with the Holy Spirit. We do that through reading and hearing Scripture.

Scripture lightens the path and fills our hearts with peace and comfort. The truth is brought back to us through this process of understanding. As it sets us free our eyes are opened to the endless possibilities of living in God's Truth.

Any vision that is given to us from God will come to pass in its' appointed time. Patience is the key factor in obtaining the full benefits of His blessings. All things have an appointed time with God because we are being prepared to receive them. God may need to remove or add some things to us so that when the blessing comes the transition will be smooth and the opposition cannot sidetrack us. In essence any hardship that we experience waiting on the blessing is a blessing itself. The true identity behind the hardship is to exalt you to yet another level in your life.

If God shows you that you will be promoted believe it. It doesn't matter that you were laid off all that matters is that you were given the vision. Your promotion may come in the form of a new job with a new employer or even starting your own business. The main thing is you must keep your faith strong with the Word. The current situation is not the true identity of the blessing.

Just because the situation doesn't physically suggest the promotion in your career doesn't mean God is not willing that into your life. During that time it's important you continue to witness about His Goodness until it comes to pass. Understand that only in the right moment will His Will happen in your life.

While you're waiting make sure you're still working and moving in the direction that God wants for you. Allow the time that you're waiting for things to happen to be the time that you get your priorities in order. Your life is shifting in a new direction and you want to make sure that you shift with it.

Continue praying so that you remain insightful on your situation. ***Amos 3:7 (ESV) "For the Lord God does nothing without revealing his secret to his servants and prophets."*** Trust Him every step of the way. Make sure that as you continue moving forward there are believers and nonbelievers waiting to bear witness of God's goodness. Give Him the glory for all the changes in your life and wait for Him to guide you during the process.

When the Vision is Unclear

After three months of searching for employment I had finally landed a job at a radiology office. I felt the weight of the world being lifted from my shoulders and was happy with the blessing. However, the feelings of relief were short lived. The office was filled with drama and things at home just seemed to be getting worse by the day. I didn't know what to make of my life.

I was faithful to God and stayed in the Word but things just weren't letting up. As soon as I thought I was in a good place everything would come crashing down around me. My marriage was at its lowest point and aside from the stress in general the late night arguments until 5 or 6 in the morning were taking a toll on me. My performance began to lack and my attendance wasn't any better.

The storm was upon me. There I was the only one outside of the office looking, hoping, praying that it wouldn't hit. I don't know how I made it inside but the entire office was in shambles. My boss and I sat there staring at one another in deep conversation. I didn't protest I only nodded my head in agreement. My time there was up. I was unemployed once again. Only this time I didn't feel stressed and I wasn't mournful. I needed the break. I wanted the break. I knew it was my time to rest.

I woke up from the dream glancing over at the clock. I hopped out of bed knowing I was going to be late for work again. I made it into the office two minutes past the time my shift started. I had been warned the day before about tardiness. I hoped no one noticed me slipping in. Midway through the day I was called into the office and despite the fact that I liked my employer and she liked me she had to let me go due to my attendance.

Strangely enough I wasn't upset. To be honest I wasn't surprised either, God had shown me this in my dream the night before. I actually felt relieved that I didn't have to dedicate anymore of my time to the job. The first thing I did when I got home was dive into my Bible. I hungered for the Word of God. There had been so much mess going on inside the office I had been spiritually drained. I needed quality time with my Father to regroup.

I was waist deep in the middle of nowhere with tornadoes closing in from all directions. There was a village of people behind me that I couldn't see. I never looked back because I knew that I was there as their protection. I was supposed to cover them through the storm. The first tornado was small and changed direction rearing off to the side before it reached us.

The second was extremely large and was heading directly towards us.

I took in every twist and turn it made, studying it, sizing up the natural disaster preparing for battle. We didn't have shelter but we had each other. I instructed everyone to grab hold of one another's hands as we prayed coming into agreement. The tornado was approaching quickly. The winds were becoming extremely violent but our embrace was strong. I told everyone to stand firm because we were going to have to endure the storm. Just as it hit I was awakened.

I was given yet another prophetic dream. I knew that God was revealing something to me but what? My life was turned upside down for nearly ten years after that dream. I experienced a divorce, several failed relationships, the loss of two children at one time, I was jobless, homeless, had no transportation, hungry, and lost. With one thing after another plowing me to the ground I was starting to feel like giving up. I didn't know what God was trying to do in my life. I didn't think I could endure anymore.

It wasn't until 2012 that I finally began to see the sun shining through the clouds. Despite, me losing my way during the storm, God always provided me with the directions back into His Grace. In the times when I was going in the wrong direction God showed me the truth. Everything that I was doing that was wrong failed me in a way that was undeniable. There was nothing good that came out of the bad I did. I ended up wounded every time.

After I became sick and tired of being sick and tired I started to question myself. My mind was telling me there had to be more to life than hurting. Then I started to remember what worked for me before. I remembered the dream, the revelation that was given to me from God. I understood that there was peace of mind and strength even when everything around me seemed chaotic. I felt His Power consuming me, building me up one atom at a time. He told me I was going to go through some serious changes but I was going to endure, I was going to be alright, if I just held on to Christ and stood firm in the body of Christ I would still be standing.

Slowly but surely God began to reveal what and who was real and wasn't. I let go of everything that was an illusion and didn't mean my family anything but harm. When I was able to let go He started adding to me. If I ever fell short on money, miraculously I'd have money come in that I wasn't even expecting. When I was sad about something, He had a way of bringing someone into my life who gave me words of encouragement and hope. There were even times when I started feeling sorry for myself and He showed me how things could be worse. The vision that was unclear started to become crisp. I saw that the Vision was manifested through His Love. There was no way I could've made it through losing my brother, my babies, my marriage, jobs, home, etc. without His Love.

Keima A. Campbell

Showing God's Love

As I stood at the gas pump I noticed a woman pulling up next to me. Her car was filled to the brim with what looked like bags of clothes and there was a small child in the back strapped in a car seat. She looked tired and worn like she hadn't slept in days. I didn't want to seem rude by staring so I turned my attention back to pumping gas.

I noticed the young lady approaching me from the corner of my eye. I redirected my attention towards her standing upright preparing myself to greet her. I gave her a warm smile as I looked her over making sure I wasn't in any danger and this would be a peaceful exchange. The "world" could be weird like that sometimes one minute there's peace and the next war.

The closer she got however the less alert I became. Her spirit was soft and delicate. As she began to speak my heart started to fill with compassion and love towards her. She told me that she wasn't from Atlanta and had recently been evicted from her apartment because she'd lost her job. Her baby was sick and they'd just come from an overnight stay in the hospital. I glanced at her car looking at her son. His leg was so tiny and frail with a hospital bracelet wrapped around it.

Turning my attention back to the young lady I noticed tears falling from her eyes. She was trying to convince me she wasn't a beggar. She apologized for approaching me but she was desperate. Her son had just gotten approved for emergency Medicaid and she needed $10 to get his prescription from the pharmacy. In that moment I saw an opportunity to show God's Everlasting Love. I seen myself in her and although I didn't have much I knew it was crucial that I helped her. She was depending on her faith to get her through this ordeal.

In that moment I realized how important it was to be a vessel for God. He was using me to give this woman hope. I wasn't in a great financial position myself at the time but I also understood the power that came with believing. I disregarded my financial situation because compared to hers I was truly blessed and her need was much greater than mine.

Matthew 6:33 "But seek first the kingdom of God and His righteousness, and all these things will be added to you." I told her to wait next to my van and proceeded into the gas station. I walked to the ATM taking out more than what she needed. When I handed her the money she attempted to decline telling me that I was giving her too much. I hadn't been evicted from my home, my children were in good health, and I had a job and gas money and food in the refrigerator. But she had nothing but the hope she was holding on to.

I told her that she needed to take all that I was giving her. I explained that the extra money was for food and somewhere to stay for the night. She thanked me but I pointed to the heavens because had God not blessed me with the means and touched my heart I wouldn't have been able to bless her in return. She was now a witness. She had confirmation that He is a loving and caring provider. She saw Him living inside of me. I too learned a lesson. That lesson was how to truly show God's Love.

Because I chose to be a blessing to this young lady, God in return blessed me. That act of kindness and love was the same as tithing or giving a sacrifice to God. I took from the small amount I had cheerfully and did Kingdom Work. In doing that I was blessed. The Lord worked out my own living arrangement. For, **Luke 6:38 (ESV) "Give, and it will be given to you. Good measure, pressed down, shaken together, running over, will be put into your lap. For with the measure you use it will be measured back to you."**

There's Power in Vision

Our true strength comes from following Jesus. It is Jesus that gives us this new life. In this new life comes the insight that was once lost. There is no more suffering because the Spirit that is dwelling inside of us knows that suffering only creates endurance. The key to life is allowing adversity to become our greatest strength.

We're able to hold on longer because of what we see through our spiritual eyes. Our faithfulness brings us the Holy Spirit which then consumes us with the power of overcoming. We overcome because of the realization that the only vision that matters is God's.

It's God's tests we are passing. We need these tests because of our testimony. Our testimony is seen by believers and nonbelievers who have been watching us. These are the people who couldn't see a way out for us until God pulled us through it. The only thing they saw was our "blind" faith. They thought it was the end of the road for us. Some may have even considered us to be crazy. However, they didn't see the vision that we saw because they weren't moving in the Spirit. They didn't trust the Truth in His Word. Therefore they couldn't see the lifeline that God had thrown out to us.

When they saw the outcome of His vision because of our faith, they believed. They saw that it didn't matter what the doctor told us, we were going to live and that's what happened. There is power in seeing what God has in store for us. We refuse to give up. We refuse to lose. If we see it as our end then that's what it will be. But, if we see it as His Will, Thy Will be done on earth as it is in Heaven.

Week Nine

Ingredients

- Bible
- Notebook
- Pencil/Pen
- Fruits/Vegetables
- Bathing Water
- Drinking Water
- Time
- Commitment
- Faith
- Trust

Psalm 145:15 (ESV) "The eyes of all look to you, and you give them their food in due season."

Keeping our eyes on the prize is essential to the very air that we breathe. Without God's vision we are unable to see the true meaning of life. And like the eye liner we use to make our eyes wider our relationship with God gives us sight better than even 20/20 vision. The eye shadow that brings the color and fun to our eyes is like the faith that brings on brighter days. Trust in the Lord and don't try to figure this thing out all on your own. Know that when your season is here, God will provide you with everything that you need and more.

Day 1 Journaling

Look at yourself in the mirror. What do you see? Is this the vision you have for yourself? If not, why do you believe you view yourself in this light? If you are satisfied with who you are looking at in the mirror do you believe that God too is satisfied with what He sees?

Day 2 Journaling

Philippians 2:3-4 (ESV) "Do nothing from rivalry or conceit, but in humility count others more significant than yourselves. Let each of you look not only to his own interests, but also to the interests of others."

Is there any area in your life where you find yourself trying to compete with someone else? What is it about the person or situation that makes you feel as if you need to be in competition? How can you do better at being selfless and looking at situations of others through the eyes of God?

Day 3 Journaling

Let's focus solely on helping someone we know is in need today. Even if it's a word of encouragement, a hug, or a smile. How did that make you feel? How did it make them feel? How do you think it may have made them feel?

Day 4 Journaling

Psalm 138:8 (ESV) "The Lord will fulfill his purpose for me; your steadfast love, O Lord, endures forever. Do not forsake the work of your hands."

Speak this Scripture over yourself today. When you speak this Scripture you are asking God to continue what He started inside of you. We may not be able to see right away where we are headed however when we ask God to reveal what He has for us He will do just that. In your journal write about what you believe God is working out in your life right now.

Day 5 Journaling

Are you looking up or down? Where does the light shine the brightest on you? How can you further bring God's Light into your everyday life?

Day 6 Journaling

Do you feel as if the burdens of life have lightened since you started on your path to righteousness? Can you see where God is leading you? Is your path more clear in this 9th week towards becoming a virtuous woman?

Day 7 Journaling

John 14:26 (ESV) "But the Helper, the Holy Spirit,

whom the Father will send in my name, he will teach you all things and bring to your remembrance all that I have said to you."

Have you noticed having any moments in which you received insight on a situation that you had looked at totally differently in the past? Are you finding healing and understanding in the past events of your life? If so, how? Thank God for continued vision into your purpose.

TO SPEAK LIFE
(10)
We're Held Accountable For Our Words

Working in a call center at times I'd get phone calls from people who were extremely upset. They'd scream, holler, and speak to me in a degrading manner. The more that happened the more I started to hate my job. The words that were being spoken to me were manifesting into my life and making it a living hell. I hated to clock into work each day because of the dreadfulness I knew I'd experience because of what someone else said to me.

In business it's quite easy for some to say, "It's just a job, don't take it personal," but the fact of the matter is what we say to or about someone is very personal. There are many instances in the old and new testament that back up the notion that we are not supposed to speak negatively towards one another. Why one might ask? The Simplest answer is, words hurt and it takes a long time to heal from them.

So many times I hear people using phrases such as, "I'm just keeping it real," or "real talk," and even, "I only speak the truth." However the words that come from their mouths are words of hate, envy, jealousy, anger, and so forth. Recklessly speaking is not keeping it real. Exposing the pain and hurt of other human beings' circumstances is not "keeping it real." It means you're speaking in ignorance.

Then what's, "keeping it real"? Have you ever thought of the meaning behind the word real? It's an adjective which means true, existing or occurring as fact; genuine; not counterfeit, artificial, or imitation; authentic. At least according to the dictionary that's what it means. With that being said, isn't it safe to say that just because you have information about one's circumstances or situation doesn't mean you're speaking truth or keeping it real when it pertains to the individual?

Hasn't it been established that God being the Owner of Truth is the Only One able to "keep it real"? The only way to keep it real is to be in communion with God. The only words that are real that come from our mouths are the words that the Holy Spirit encourages us to speak.

The Bible tells us to look to God for help in all things that we do. This is especially true when speaking words into the atmosphere and over the lives of ourselves and others. We don't want to attach ourselves to the words people say to or about us, but in reality we do. The words we speak to one another are extremely powerful. What comes out of our mouths promotes either life or death.

The Bible says that we're held accountable for every word we speak. One day we'll have go before the Lord to explain what we've said to or about someone. Think about some things you've said. Do you believe Our Father is happy with the words you've spoken over your brothers and sisters in Christ?

One of my children used to have a lot of behavioral problems. She'd fight and argue with others constantly. The things she'd say to others hurt them just as much as her striking them.

When she'd get chastised she'd say, "I'm so bad! I hate myself!" I'd tell her there's no such thing as a "bad person" there's only bad decisions. I explained to her that she could change if she truly wanted to but it all started with her. The first thing she'd have to do was stop labeling herself as "bad".

In addition to speaking this over my daughter I had to speak life over my family members as well. Some of them had instilled that deadly thinking into her very existence. They'd hear about something she'd done and label her as "bad". I don't believe they said this to hurt or degrade her in anyway but it did. The truth is no matter how you slice it bad is just bad. It's never good.

The words that were spoken over her started to manifest into the atmosphere. It was like a curse all caused from negatively speaking to and about her. I refused to accept that for my child otherwise; her future would've been in very "bad" shape.

This happens to so many people. Children who are bullied, teased, abused become introverted and tend to have low self-esteem because of words. Well into adulthood they find it hard to be successful in many areas of their lives. They become sad, depressed, or get into relationships that are abusive and hurtful because subconsciously they believe that's what they deserve. They can become hardened and hurt others with no regard.

Our words can shape the entire life of someone else. This is why it's very important to ask God to fill us with His Spirit. His Spirit then guides us throughout the day. We need that guidance in directing us and what we put out into the world.

Visualize everything that is going on around you. How many of us have bought into the notion that we're free? If we continue to believe in that lie although our flesh consistently enjoys the fruits of sin with no regard, then we'll continue to find ourselves in hurtful situations. We'll constantly search outside of ourselves looking for a way out. Some of us may even tell ourselves that we're happy, and smile big for that invisible camera, but behind closed doors the tears will fall. They will flow effortlessly because of the front we put on for everyone else.

Because of lies we never get the healing and the help we need to overcome our inner demons. What others spoke over us and what we spoke to ourselves stick with us day after day until the lie we've been holding on to feels like it's a part of our very being. The lie causes us turmoil, it's our demise.

In order for the words that we speak to be acceptable to God first and foremost they can't be a lie. Someone once told me, "The truth hurts," and I believed that statement for a very long time. Then

God began to enlighten me, exposing the lies I had been taught all my life.

See the truth never hurts. Truth allows you to grow and become perfected in God. It's the lie that covers the truth that hurts. When we're unaware of where the truth comes from we can never come to know it in its purest form. The Word of God says that the truth sets us free. Think about that statement.

The truth sets us free because His burden is light. If we are speaking and walking in His Truth then we are living righteously. **Ephesians 4:29 (ESV) "Let no corrupting talk come out of your mouths, but only such as is good for building up, as fits the occasion, that it may give grace to those who hear."** Every single word that comes from our mouths should be uplifting to the Kingdom of God. This is the only speech that is acceptable to God.

The function of God's Kingdom is love and when we love one another we come together to give each other hope and encouragement. Words are powerful, more powerful than even actions at times.

The whole point of speaking is to convey information, a thought, an opinion, or feeling about something. If we are guided by the Holy Spirit of God every bit of information that comes to mind and everything that we feel is good. When I say "good" I mean these things are morally right. Things that were meant to tear us down have no power over us because of what's living inside of us.

When living in a world filled with hurt and pain,

it's mandatory that our words are used only for the building up of the people. We must speak life. We can't pretend to be walking with God if we aren't allowing Him to shine through us. We can't be Christian women and yet we're tearing others down with our words. We're merely servants of the Most High God and we must present ourselves as such in the way we walk, talk, and the things we do even behind closed doors.

When we're testifying, preaching, and teaching to one another we have to be courteous of those who are listening. We can't be focused on ourselves and what we believe. Our focus must be on accomplishing God's Will. This doesn't mean that we have to condone any sin that we see being committed. This merely means we have to show correction through the Love of God's Word. We don't focus on the sin, we focus on the salvation that Jesus gives to us sinners.

The only acceptable speech is speech filled with Love. Love doesn't judge, it's not selfish or self-righteous, prideful, nor arrogant. Love's the opposite of all those things and endures even the most trying trials and tribulations. Love will give perfect peace to the giver and receiver. Beautiful words are like fresh spring water. They cleanse and wash away the impurities of our souls. The Word was made flesh that flesh was Jesus; following His path is the only way to communicate in Spirit and Truth to others.

Affirmations

Every word spoken provokes thought and every

action starts out as a thought. As women of virtue we have to be sure to encourage others into thinking about the Word. If we can think the Word, we can speak it, if we can speak it we will live it, and when we live we have become it.

This is why affirmation is so important in living a Christian lifestyle. We not only should affirm ourselves but others as well. The greatest thing about each of us is this, if we are here searching for answers, God has already called us to be disciples. **Matthew 28:19 (ESV) "Go therefore and make disciples of all nations, baptizing them in the name of the Father and of the Son and of the Holy Spirit."** As a Disciple of Christ we are given authority to speak the gospel on behalf of God through the Holy Spirit. We are to motivate and encourage others to live this same lifestyle and boldly speak the Word of God to the masses.

We can only accomplish this through fulfilling and becoming who God intended for us to be. In many instances we may have lost sight as to what our true being is. It's our duty to "re-learn" ourselves from the inside out. We have to know and acknowledge that no matter what walk of life we come from we are here for a purpose that is higher than our own. Even if we are in the middle of some mess right now God still has a place for us in His Kingdom.

God made us in His Image and likeness. We're not perfect but are perfected through Him. Therefore we can't be failures. All the times we reduced ourselves or someone else to nothing it was an illusion. We belong to God and even when no one else can see the greatness in us God does. He made us this way!

Start speaking life over yourselves right now. Look yourself in the mirror and tell yourself that you are a woman of God. You're strong because He who loves in you is strong. You are the daughter of a loving, forgiving, merciful, and all powerful Father. Your Father loves you with no conditions. Tell yourself you are convinced that our Lord God made you in His image. Remind yourself that because you are a believer in the Son Jesus Christ you have authority over all things here on this earth. Rebuke any satanic covenant, curse, stronghold, or demonic presence attempting to place itself in your life.

Remind yourself that you were made with a purpose in mind. Acknowledge that although you have experienced trials and tribulations God has a place for you in the Kingdom. Tell yourself you're beautiful, intelligent, wise, at peace, and filled with joy and happiness. Acknowledge that the Lord will never leave you nor forsake you. Thank Him in advance for giving you the gift of salvation and for allowing His Spirit to live in you every day. Affirm yourself in the Spirit today. Right now!

Living The Word

Living this life is about talking the talk and walking the walk at the very same time. Seeing the young man who sells drugs and getting a minute of his time to give him a prophetic word from God is Living the Word. The 15 year old girl with a face full of makeup, shorts that barely cover her backside, with her breasts exposed doesn't need a side eye; she needs a prophetic Word from God through you.

The homeless person begging outside the corner store doesn't need a sneer of disapproval from you. What he needs is a prayer, some food and an encouraging Word that God's given to you. Our faith will give them faith. Our belief in God's ability to bring them out of the mess they're in gives them a glimpse of how real and compassionate this Christian lifestyle truly is.

Even if you have to give a word of hope and encouragement ten thousand times to the same person, please understand that God doesn't work on our time. He doesn't even see time. When that person is in the appropriate moment they'll get it. It isn't for us to say when that time should be. Our only job is to display the love and kindness of Christ so that people will know that God is real.

Throughout this book I have spoken about my ex-husband not necessarily in a negative way but the experiences we've had with one another. It's important for my own spiritual growth and his for me to say to all of you that he too has experienced heartache in his life. While this is not an excuse for a lot of his actions it is however the root of his old lifestyle.

With God I've been able to forgive him. In that forgiveness our relationship as parents and as brother and sister in Christ has strengthened. God has allowed me to help him in facing his past and to see everything that has happened in his life with new eyes. I feel blessed to have been able to speak life to him.

There was a time when I was very toxic and angry towards him. Each time we spoke I'd say things that I knew would hurt him to his core. I've come to understand that I was wrong. I have asked and been given his forgiveness, and I thank the Lord for that. In that forgiveness he has found peace at least when it comes to our failed marriage.

I'm truly grateful to God for that because not only did my ex-husband need healing but I needed it as well. That healing led to forgiveness and closure. As we open ourselves up to the notion of positive thinking we'll speak positivity into the atmosphere which will bring about a positive change in our lives.

Each day we must ask God to renew our Spirit. This helps us to stay focused on our walk and not on what other people are thinking or saying about us. Our actions will be the ultimate factor that will change others minds about us. God's light cannot be denied. Even when people come up against us we should bless them and keep them in our prayers.

Remember ladies we are to love everyone. We are all children of God. We don't want Our Father punishing our brothers and sisters. So we keep them in prayer even when they aren't interested in keeping the peace with us. We're not in the business of reaping and sowing a harvest that doesn't nourish our bodies. We want to eat from our crops. If we are playing tit for tat with one another we're not living life. We have then started living to die.

Matthew 26:52-54 (ESV) "Then Jesus said to him, 'Put your sword back into its place. For all who take the sword will perish by the sword. Do you think that I cannot appeal to my Father, and He will at once send me more than twelve legions of angels? But how then should the Scriptures be fulfilled, that I must be so?"

Everything that someone does to us bad or good can only happen because God allowed it to happen. It's a part of our very own Scripture for our lives. God makes no mistakes and everything that we endure is a part of God's plan. He allows us to experience life's ups and downs so that we can speak out and testify about His Goodness. When we do this we draw others closer to Him.

Take time to think about the words that you'll allow to come from your mouth from this day forward. When you're angry sit back and ponder on the situation at hand before you take action. Ask God to guide you in your actions when approaching others or a situation so that you are doing His Will and not your own. Speak life and never death. When His Word rests on your tongue it demands respect and admiration while protecting you from evil.

Week Ten

Ingredients
- Bible
- Notebook
- Pencil/Pen
- Fruits/Vegetables
- Bathing Water
- Drinking Water
- Time
- Commitment
- Faith
- Trust

Day 1 Journaling

Goal: Speak words that give life to others.
What is the purpose of this Goal?

How will you hold yourself accountable for this goal?

Day 2 Journaling

Proverbs 13:3 (ESV) "Whoever guards his mouth preserves his life; he who opens wide his lips comes to ruin."

List 7 things you can do to ensure you're speaking life to others.

Day 3 Journaling

Ephesians 4:15 (ESV) "Rather, speaking the truth in love, we are to grow up in every way into Him who is the head, into Christ,"

Make a conscious effort to speak the Gospel to someone you see struggling today. It doesn't matter how small their struggle is.

What response did you get from speaking the Truth in love?

Day 4 Journaling

1 Peter 2:9 (ESV) "But you are a chosen race, a royal priesthood, a holy nation, a people for his own possession, that you may proclaim the excellences of Him who called you out of darkness into his marvelous light."

Speak this Scripture to yourself at least seven times as you look in the mirror today. Affirm it by stating, "God said it, I believe it, and that settles it."

How did this affirmation make you feel?

Day 5 Journaling

James 1:16-18 (MSG) "So, my very dear friends, don't get thrown off course. Every desirable and beneficial gift comes out of heaven. The gifts are rivers of light cascading down from the Father of Light. There is nothing deceitful in God, nothing two-faced, nothing fickle. He brought us to life using the true Word, showing us off as the crown of all His creatures."

Think of some times in which you found yourself being two-faced or fickle towards someone else. In detail confess to Our Lord God the error of your ways and ask for forgiveness.

Make a journal entry about why speaking the Word of God is important in your personal life.

Day 6 Journaling

1 Timothy 4:12 (ESV) "Let no one despise you for your youth, but set the believers an example in speech, in conduct, in love, in faith, in purity."

List a situation where you've allowed God to shine through in your:

- Speech
- Conduct
- Love

- Faith
- Purity

In these situations how did you feel after you displayed these things to believers as well as non-believers?

What was their reaction?

If you had a chance to be a deliverer of this message again would you have allowed yourself to be used more or in a different manner?

Do you feel that God was or is pleased with how you have represented yourself on behalf of the Kingdom? Why? Why not?

Day 7 Journaling

Mark 16:15 (ESV) "And He said to them, 'Go into all the world and proclaim the gospel to the whole creation."

We talked about Faith with Works in the previous two chapters. List some ways you can introduce our brothers and sisters to Christ. How will you encourage them in their own walk?

FASHIONED BY GOD
(11)

God's Armor

Ephesians 6:10-20 (NIV) "[10] Finally, be strong in the Lord and in his mighty power. [11] Put on the full armor of God, so that you can take your stand against the devil's schemes. [12] For our struggle is not against flesh and blood, but against the rulers, against the authorities, against the powers of this dark world and against the spiritual forces of evil in the heavenly realms. [13] Therefore put on the full armor of God, so that when the day of evil comes, you may be able to stand your ground, and after you have done everything, to stand. [14] Stand firm then, with the belt of truth buckled around your waist, with the breastplate of righteousness in place, [15] and with your feet fitted with the readiness that comes from the gospel of peace. [16] In addition to all this, take up the shield of faith, with which you can extinguish all the flaming arrows of the evil one. [17] Take the helmet of salvation and the sword of the Spirit, which is the word of God. [18] And pray in the Spirit on all occasions with all kinds of prayers and requests. With this in mind, be alert and always keep on praying for all the Lord's people. [19] Pray also for me, that whenever I speak, words may be given me so that I will fearlessly make known the mystery of the gospel, [20] for which I am an ambassador in

chains. Pray that I may declare it fearlessly, as I should."

Once we've kicked the enemy out of our lives he has nowhere to go. So he searches looking for a way back in. ***1 Peter 5:8 (ESV) "Be sober-minded; be watchful. Your adversary the devil prowls around like a soaring lion, seeking someone to devour."*** That sounds very violent. To devour is to consume until there is no more. It wants to eat your soul like a lion does its' prey.

Have you ever saw how lions stalk their prey? They wait patiently, watching their preys' every move until they are least expectant of an attack. Out of nowhere the lion appears. Usually more than one as the females hunts in packs. They chase down the unsuspecting gazelle sometimes even targeting the babies. When they're caught the lions tear them apart piece by piece with no mercy until they are no more.

The dress code listed in Ephesians 6:10-20 is how we must dress every single day of our lives to avoid being devoured by the enemy. Now that we're walking with God we're going to run into a whole other set of "problems". I don't like giving too much credit to the enemy but I will say once you start changing your mind and your life the enemy will start pressing harder.

The Belt of Truth

This is why God has instructed us in this manner; Standing firm with the belt of truth buckled around our waists. We have already established that the truth will set us free. It sets our minds free which in return gives us freedom in so many other aspects of our lives.

Spiritual bondage keeps us capacitated from achieving success and receiving what God has for us. If we're free we become able to see who God has truly made us and our true potential. We're able to recognize that our lives are indeed grand. The belt of truth is wrapped around our waist or stomachs which is the core of our bodies. It is what strengthens our backbones so that we can stand tall and not become crippled and hunched over by the strong winds of life's storms.

The truth brings us into a good life. No more being bound by life's circumstances. In keeping this Truth we develop an understanding of life and are then able to help others pick up the pieces of their own. We have the ability to show them the truth in us so that they can recognize the truth in themselves.

When the Truth is in us it becomes easy to do what's right and notice the lies and deceit of the world. We start to notice things that aren't of God and steer clear from them. Sometimes those things are people and that's okay! Once you've had the opportunity to grow from God's baby girl to His young woman you'll be able to resurface and minister to those you've had to leave behind.

Luke 9:60 (ESV) "And Jesus said to him, "Leave the dead to bury their own dead. But as

for you, go and proclaim the kingdom of God."
He is speaking of the spiritually dead those who can't see the truth. But once we've grown into the women we were made to be, we can come back with the medicine needed to heal the sick and revive the dead. When the time is right we'll testify to them about life and our own resurrection.

The Breastplate of Righteousness

We know the truth now it's time to apply the truth to our lives. We must strap on the breastplate of righteousness. Everything of God is morally correct. We have to make sure those morals, values and standards are in alignment with what God see's acceptable.

We may have to suffer and sacrifice according to worldly standards because of our righteousness. We'll see people doing things that are ungodly for the sake of being rich, famous, and popular. You may be like me riding around in a minivan with two car seats. People may laugh at you because you aren't driving a luxury SUV, or living in million dollar home, or wearing $1500 shoes.

I had someone once ask me why I drove a minivan when I could have an SUV. I wasn't offended by the question, but it made me think really hard about my life. I could go out and buy a luxury vehicle or an SUV but what would I have had to do to get it? Why would having this vehicle be so important to my family and me? Did I need to appease this person who seemed to be looking down upon me because of the type of vehicle I drove?

God warns about making hasty decisions to get materialistic things. I was blessed in that moment because of my faithfulness to this lifestyle. I chose to hold God close. I was able to see the trickery in the statement. At one point in time I cared about what people thought of me. While in that same mind frame I believed that I had to get what I wanted when I wanted it. Even if it meant degrading me and stepping off of this platform that God had built specifically for me. I was willing to be removed from His Grace.

But in keeping the breastplate of righteous on to protect my heart and its desires I was able to recognize the truth. Truth is my van didn't define who I was as a person. It was my morals, values, standards, and integrity that defined me.

That breastplate protects our hearts from desires that are not of our natural state but of the flesh. God said, "He would give us what we desire." Our hearts are what desire things and it has to be in the right place to receive what it should. It has to be unhardened to reap the full benefits of what should be desirable. Otherwise we fall into practices that hurt us by unarming us and leaving us open and ready to be devoured.

Peaceful Footsteps

Our feet are covered in peace. God is ordering our steps. He does this so that no matter what situation we're faced with we can walk through it with a calmness that others will never be able to understand, unless they've already experienced it. When you're walking in peace you don't get anxious and upset when things don't look how you believe they should look. In signs of trouble you're able to pray and submit to God because you know and understand that He is still in control.

John 16:33 (ESV) "I have said these things to you, that in me you may have peace. In the world you will have tribulation. But take heart; I have overcome the world." There's so much going on all at same time. If we focus on everything around us our lives become as chaotic as the world we live in. But, if we keep our minds on God, we're given peace of mind. Trust is being built so that our faithfulness and obedience in following Jesus Christ allows Him to overcome the world through us.

The Shield of Faith

We have on our shield of faith to keep us from wavering and becoming weary. At this point we know that we'll receive everything that we ask for in the name of Jesus as long as we believe. God is happy with us as we've become friends and daughters over time. Not only did He give us life and send us into this world but He gave us who we needed to overcome the world. That was Jesus Christ.

We're working every single day ministering to the world about the greatness of God. We're spreading the Good News about Jesus and what following and trusting in Him has done in our own lives and what this lifestyle will do for theirs. As our faith reflects our works and our works reflects our faith even we become more convinced of this goodness. The things that we do for good keeps us from doing the things the devil wants us to do for bad.

As we continue on this journey that is led by faith we grow in authority and power. Because the Spirit of God is living and moving inside of us we can move mountains. We have the authority to heal the sick, drive out demons, and perform an entire host of miracles to show He is all powerful.

Wearing the Helmet of Salvation

The Helmet of salvation is what keeps us sane in the middle of all of this. Salvation saves our souls from condemnation. It was salvation that allowed us to be exonerated from the death sentence of our sins. Salvation is what wiped away the dirty burdens of sin and washed us with the blood making us clean without a spot on us.

That act of salvation not only saved us from death but it taught us how to forgive. Forgiveness is the greatest sense of empowerment we can ever have over our lives. It releases so much of the burdens we tend to place on ourselves. Forgiveness itself gives us the freedom to experience real unadulterated joy in our lives.

When we smile we are smiling not because we have to put on a show but because we're truly happy. We have a new life. Born again literally means that we have a fresh start and in that fresh start we have a fresh and new mind. So we can't and shouldn't make any excuses as to why we aren't following the Word of God.

Even when we make mistakes we shall repent never looking back or beating ourselves over the heads about old stupid decisions. Remember that was the old you and this is the new you. So yes you might make a mistake and that mistake may have followed you from your past. But God no longer sees any of that.

He only sees this new mistake and is waiting for repentance and for you to move on. There's no need to dwell on the sin. We dwell only on the goodness of our Lord. **Romans 8:1 (ESV) "There is therefore now no condemnation for those who are in Christ Jesus."** You aren't condemned for your mistakes because you're wearing your helmet of salvation.

The Sword of the Spirit

The last thing we need is our sword. This sword represents the Word of God. I noticed in my life now when I sense that someone is becoming argumentative with me when I give them the Word of God and they retreat. On rare occasions they're extremely hostile accusing me of being judgmental. In my own defense, I am aware that I'm holy and the Bible doesn't prevent those who are holy from passing judgment. However, it's up to the holy to judge not being judgmental but with understanding, compassion, empathy, and gentleness.

Sometimes, I have no clue why the person I'm communicating with has become so angry. None the less I'm able to see the deceit in what's going on. The enemy is cunning. When Jesus was in the wilderness he tried to convince the Son of God to abandon all that God had instilled in Him and experience the "world". If he tried to convince Jesus believe he will try to convince you to abandon all that God has instilled in you as well.

The Word of God said the Holy Spirit dwells inside of you. Your body is its temple. Now understand when you are filled with the Spirit it never goes away. Have you ever done something that you knew was wrong and although you did it anyway afterwards you felt bad? That's because the Holy Spirit grieves inside of us who are filled when we do the wrong things. Because, the Spirit is in us we have to keep our temple filled and renewed daily by staying in the Word, praying, and developing a personal relationship with the Father.

If the enemy should rise up against you understand you are not fighting against flesh and blood. Slay him with the Word of God. Don't argue, fuss, or fight use the One thing that only God can give you. This is the only thing that will teach you all the things of the world and of heavenly places. That is the Holy Spirit, your sword.

You see arguing with other people isn't godly. When you have an argument it affects your mental, spiritual, and physical wellbeing in a negative way. Arguing and fighting back takes you out of your state of holiness. Keep away from resorting to worldly ways when handling these issues. Therefore, speak the Word which is always positive and righteous. It will counteract the negativity that comes from the adversary.

Whoever hears His Words are blessed. After you've put the Word of God into the atmosphere you're safe. You may not see the benefits of allowing the Spirit to speak through you in that moment, but the seed has been planted inside all who heard it.

Insight through Hindsight

As I reflect on my life I can remember a very dark time period where I was angry about everything. I would be upset about something that should've brought me to my knees, but it didn't. It should have made me cry but instead I'd be filled with rage. It was as if I had literally run out of tears. I didn't feel anything at all. I thought I had no heart. My heart had turned to stone.

Our worth is determined by what is acceptable to God. This armor keeps us in check because it covers us from head to toe. God doesn't want us running around here being envious of one another and speaking death into each other's lives.

Therefore our spiritual house needs to be in order. We have to steer clear of all sin because of who we are. We're made in His Image and as long as we keep Him at the forefront we're winning. God cannot sin. We are His chosen children not some of us but all of us. Jesus died to save everyone in this world.

Song of Solomon 4:7 (NIV) "You are altogether

beautiful, my darling; there is no flaw in you."
You see when God is dwelling inside of you He does not see you as flawed. He sees you for who He made you to be. Although through our flesh we are weak through Him we have mighty strength. Through Him we're made perfect as we hold on tight to His Word and never let go.

When God entered my life He gave me a new spirit. He softened me to a point that now I cry about everything. It's okay with me because it's more like a cleansing session every time I release my tears. My tears seem to give me added strength. They are no longer tears of despair, heartache, and pain but of thankfulness, hope, and faith. Through my tears I praise Him and can see His greatness.

In following Jesus we're able to become compassionate like our Father. Our hearts are pulled in the direction of love towards one another and not hate, envy, or jealousy. As our hearts open we become more like God in the decisions that we make. We're designed to have this God Intelligence. So when we're faithful in following Jesus we start to remember the knowledge we'd obtained before we were even formed in our mothers' wombs.

God's knowledge is like learning a foreign language. If you don't use it you'll lose it. So we continuously seek insight from Scripture and direct relationship with Him. He's happy to give us all the tools we need to live a wonderful life even here on earth. No parent wants their child to be miserable. He's always just a conversation away.

The more we converse with Him the easier it is to follow in His footsteps. We know we are on the right path because we feel it deep down inside of our souls. We're no longer conflicted with the things that we say or do. We have this newfound confidence about ourselves.

I myself was always shy about sharing my writing. I was unsure about my skill as a writer, my thoughts, and feelings being shared with others. Here I am this is my third published book. My books are available to the world. I have emails that come in from fans and questions on Facebook, and even Twitter. I'm able to communicate like I've never been able to communicate before. I've always had something to say but was never totally comfortable in saying it. Now, I have no fear of what I speak to someone. Because, I know that I'm saying are the right things.

Isaiah 41:10 (ESV) *"Fear not, for I am with you; be not dismayed, for I am your God; I will strengthen you, I will help you, I will uphold you with my righteous hand."* When I read that Scripture I get so excited because I've witnessed this first hand. Not because, I'm Keima but because God is good for no reason at all.

His Word has allowed me to reach heights I never could've reached on my own as human being. I had a gentlemen contact me who had a multitude of credentials. He himself was writing a book but wanted to know how much I would charge him to guide him through the entire process of writing, self-publishing, marketing, etc. I asked him what the book was about and he gave me an overview of this amazing project. I was convicted to share my plunders and successes with him free of charge.

Keima would have been intimidated by this man because he was an accomplished businessman and very wise regarding life in general. Now what's truly amazing is God's ability to supernaturally place us in positions of authority in situations we rule ourselves out of. He'd already helped me to overcome the uncertainty of speaking to others and now He was placing me right where I needed to be to move forward in my ministry.

I keep saying me but understand I don't get any of the credit. I know that all of this is because I've allowed the Spirit to do in me what It wants to do. It's been waiting to do this for a very long time. Little by little I've been getting the assurance I needed to come into the virtuous woman I am destined to be. One small piece at a time I've been put together in a manner that Versace himself couldn't place on a runway anywhere in this world.

2 Corinthians 3:5 (ESV) *"Not that we are sufficient in ourselves to claim anything as coming from us, but our sufficiency is from God."*

There are many traits that need to be developed before we can come into who we really are as women of God. Some of those traits we develop very easily and some we'll have to work diligently on and that's okay. When we start taking responsibility for our lives we become better at living. Keep pressing forward my sisters with all that is inside of you. If you do you won't ever fall.

When God has shown you who you are believe Him. Remember when Peter and the other disciples saw Jesus walking on water during the storm? At first they were afraid but Jesus told them to not be afraid it was him. They couldn't believe that He was walking on water. Peter set out after Jesus calling after him to walk on the water as well. He became distracted and afraid when things started looking a little rough in the eye of the storm and he took his eyes off of Jesus. As soon as he did so he started to sink. He was drowning!

But Jesus caught him. When He caught him he told him this, "You of little faith. Why did you doubt?" You can find that statement in **Matthew 14:31,** had Peter not doubted, had he kept his eyes on Jesus, he would've never started to sink. Had he understood the power that God had over his life through His Son he could have saved himself from that traumatic experience.

God will make a way out of no way. It's only possible for miracles to manifest in our lives when we are in accordance with Him. One body, the body of Christ and one mind, God Intelligence. The wind was the test of faith for Peter and Jesus' ability to save Peter from himself was confirmation that God is real and can make a way even in impossible situations.

The power is inside of us if we allow it to reside there. He's waiting for us to say it's okay Father, have your way with me. Any uncertainty that I have, I place it in your hands because I know that you are my strength.

John 10:30 (ESV) "I and the Father are one." When I hear that Scripture it gives me so much joy, faith, and hope, Jesus was referring to the fact that Him and the Father are the same. If we make up the body of Jesus (Christ) then that means we too are the same as the Father. Correct? That means anything is possible for us. That means when people speak out against us it doesn't matter because of God's power. God's power overrides any other power on this earth.

The light always illuminates darkness so that we can see. We are blessed to be made in His image. We should respect ourselves in everything that we do as we are a representation of God Himself. The way we dress should reflect the way God see's us. Although our clothing doesn't make us who we are it does show others what state of mind we are in.

The decisions we make as individuals illicit behaviors. If we demand respect in how we present ourselves there is no need to get into mundane arguments over someone disrespecting us. If we go outside with our behinds hanging out of our shorts or a skin tight outfit that shows every curve of our body others are going to notice us. That notoriety however will be in a negative light. They will see us as sexual objects and not women of God. Should they judge us by the way we look? No, but the truth of the matter is people do.

To avoid the unnecessary stress of dealing with the ignorance of others we have to keep our eyes on God. That means fully representing His essence that is inside of us. ***1 Timothy 2:9-10 (ESV) "Likewise*** *also that women should adorn themselves in respectable apparel, with modesty and self-control, not with braided hair and gold or pearls or costly attire, but with what is proper for women who profess godliness—with good works."*

I know some of you are saying what? Let me explain to you this Scripture as this information is coming directly from the Holy Spirit. The basis of this Scripture is modesty in what we wear. Anything that is used to draw attention to you due to sexual undertones is unacceptable.

In the Bible women who wore makeup and dressed a certain way to get attention were prostitutes. I'm not saying because you dress a certain way that you won't be blessed or favored by God. Truth is He says to come as you are. You're going to draw an entirely different type of people to find out who He is. As we grow and develop our views change. Ideals of what we should look like and how we should carry ourselves change too. Modesty and humbleness will begin to take over.

Before you decide that you'd like to wear a certain outfit, jewelry, etc. ask yourself why am I wearing this? What is the result I hope to achieve from putting this on? What do I think the designer is trying to sell to the world with this article of clothing? Is this thought process conducive with what God wants for me and what God means to me? As women we should question these things as we go out into the world.

Week Eleven

Ingredients
- Bible
- Notebook
- Pencil/Pen
- Fruits/Vegetables
- Bathing Water
- Drinking Water
- Time
- Commitment
- Faith
- Trust

    Close your eyes and envision yourself in the presence of God Himself. Breathe and allow His Love to consume you. Thank Him for renewing your Spirit and for opening your heart to receive all that He has for you over these past ten weeks. Now imagine your reward. Did you see it? Do you believe it? I do! I agree with the vision God has given you for your life and your ministry.

In this last week I think it's important that we take a stroll down memory lane. Pull out your responses to the questions at the beginning of the book and answer them again.

- Who am I?
- Who do I hope to become?
- What do I think I will gain from this book?

- What are the goals I will set for myself to become a better me?
- When will I start transforming my life?
- When do I hope to start seeing the results of this transformation?
- Where in my life will these changes take place?
- Where will I go from here?
- Why do I feel the need to make changes in my life?
- Why is it important that I have a core set of values, standards, and morals?
- How do I represent myself as a virtuous woman now?
- How will I represent myself as a virtuous woman in the future?

Has your answers changed? Do you see growth since the beginning of this journey? I pray that all of you enjoyed this book. I also pray that you were given insight and encouragement in reading it. I truly look forward to receiving your emails in the future. Be absolutely blessed.

The Makeup of a Virtuous woman

ABOUT THE AUTHOR

Keima Campbell has been writing for more than twenty years. She'd published a couple secular books before God changed her path and led her to write only for His Kingdom. She has taken pride in writing her first autobiography/ self-help book called, The Makeup of a Virtuous Woman allowing herself to become transparent and encourage women to lay their burdens upon God for freedom in all areas of their lives. She currently lives in Atlanta, GA with her four children and has recently taken on a couple new ventures such as Public Speaking and Christian Life Coaching. She is also working on a few new projects encouraging the growth of God's Kingdom. To reach her feel free to contact her at Authorkeimacampbell@gmail.com.